Contents

Supporting Black Pupils and Parents

The persistence of the achievement gap and high exclusion rates of Black children in the UK and elsewhere highlight an urgent need to improve the way their teaching and learning is supported in today's schools. Teachers often blame parents, parents blame teachers, and an unhappy downward spiral ensues.

Drawing on her extensive experience, Lorna Cork here explores the day-to-day needs and expectations of Black parents and their children in education. She focuses on contemporary situations and uses real-life case studies to emphasise the human consequences of the issues behind the statistics.

This comprehensive and lively text looks in detail at five key organisations that exist to support Black parents. It examines their home–school interventions and discusses the central issues arising out of their efforts with twenty Black families. This wide body of fascinating evidence offers fresh perspectives, providing much needed advice and guidance to all those seeking to improve co-operation between Black families and schools. Constructive in tone, whilst not shirking 'uncomfortable' challenges, this book provides examples of good practice and strategies that have been tried and tested, as well as suggestions for further reading and additional sources of support.

Any education professional – teacher, student teacher or staff at an LEA – in addition to anyone with a serious interest in race issues, is sure to find this essential reading.

Dr Lorna Cork is currently an education adviser with a large, inner-city LEA.

Supporting Black Pupils and Parents

Understanding and improving home–school relations

Dr Lorna Cork

With a foreword by Doreen Lawrence

Routledge
Taylor & Francis Group

LONDON AND NEW YORK

First published 2005 by Routledge
2 Park Square, Milton Park, Abingdon, Oxon OX14 4RN

Simultaneously published in the USA and Canada
by Routledge
270 Madison Ave, New York, NY 10016

Transferred to Digital Printing 2006

Routledge is an imprint of the Taylor & Francis Group, an informa business

© 2005 Lorna Cork

Typeset in Sabon by
GreenGate Publishing Services, Tonbridge, Kent
Printed and bound in Great Britain by
TJI Digital, Padstow, Cornwall

British Library Cataloguing in Publication Data
A catalogue record for this book is available from the British Library

Library of Congress Cataloging in Publication Data
Supporting Black pupils : understanding and improving home-school
relations / Lorna Cork.
    p. cm.
Includes bibliographical references and index.
1. Students, Black–Social conditions. 2. Home and school. 3.
Parent-teacher relationships. 4. Discrimination in education. I. Title.

LC2699.C67 2005
371.829'96041–dc22

2004023868

ISBN 10: 0-415-34056-X (cased)
ISBN 10: 0-415-34055-1 (limp)

ISBN 13: 978-0-415-34056-4 (cased)
ISBN 13: 978-0-415-34055-7 (limp)

Foreword

Doreen Lawrence

This book gives an account of research carried out on the experiences of Black parents and their children in the British education system. The research highlights Black parents' concerns about their children's education: the fact that their children are underachieving in schools today and the fact that there have been few changes since the early 1960s when this was first highlighted. One of the first reports that came out was about sink schools and how Black children were made educationally subnormal by racism and the collective failure of the educational system.

This research by Lorna Cork sets out the difficulties encountered by many Black parents and their children. The struggles that are faced on a daily basis in schools sometimes can be seen to come from the teachers themselves.

The research looks at ways of supporting parents and their children in and out of schools by working with agencies that work with schools to find a way forward that is beneficial for all. The agencies try to find a middle ground so that there are no losers. This is shown to be done by providing the opportunities where both parents and teachers can work together for the pupils.

The research also highlights some of the problems in our schools that are not new for Black pupils and their parents because they (the parents) too had the same experiences when they faced racism and discrimination as pupils.

The reality of Black children failing in school, as I have said, has been well documented for the past forty years and one could say that nothing much has changed. In order for Black children to gain access to all levels of the British workforce, parents and members of the Black community must make it their duty to play an active part in their children's education; also to make sure that their children acquire the skills necessary to take their rightful place in the workforce and for the educational system to provide the necessary access in education to allow this to happen.

The role of Black mothers came through strongly in the research; the sacrifices made by them to obtain education and then invest in their children's future are enormous. Black parents have had to use strategies in order to help children to survive in the school setting. The need to overcome barriers faced on a daily basis can be soul-destroying. The negativity of many white teachers leads the way and can impact on Black children as a whole, and that in turn leads to underachieving. In many cases it is due to not understanding the feelings of Black parents, regardless of their background, and this in turn affects Black children's achievement levels in school.

What came across strongly from the research were the clear messages that schools have a duty to provide protection for children in the learning environment that they are studying in. What is lacking for Black pupils are the relevant materials that would specifically provide positive images of those from their own background. We all need role models to aspire to and that is what is missing for many Black children in the school environment.

The overwhelming messages in the research from Black parents are about having the right support for themselves and their children; having the right organisation that understands and provides support for their needs and that is willing to address issues in a more holistic way that would enable achievement more effectively.

This research has demonstrated in more ways than one that focusing on Black parents, and their concerns for their children in achieving the level of education that they are entitled to, can be beneficial to society as whole.

Acknowledgements

It is particularly fitting given the subject matter of the book to start with an acknowledgement to my Jamaican-born mother, in recognition of her continued support, guidance and unfailing faith in me, the Black community and the human race. Thanks Mum, for truly being the backbone of our family and the example you have shown to me and many others in the family and the wider community. My sisters Collette and Andrea and my brother Rupert, you have been more helpful than you realise. I am especially grateful to you, Collette, for your practical, frank and quick response to my moments of writer's doubts. To my husband Carl and all the family here and across the diaspora, including the various 'aunts' and 'uncles', I appreciate your encouragement. Thank you to the many friends and colleagues who continue to support my personal and professional growth and have encouraged me to write this book – you know who you are and it doesn't seem fair to single out one particular individual.

I am indebted to Professor Donald McIntyre for the academically rigorous, good-humoured, open and culturally sensitive manner of his supervision of the thesis on which this book is based. Donald, I appreciate the confidence you have displayed in the academic abilities of this 'non-traditional' Cambridge student which continues in the way you have urged me to complete this book. Likewise, I would like to thank Routledge for taking me on board as a first-time author and Alison Foyle in particular for the prompt and encouraging response to my initial proposal. The patience shown by the editorial assistants and the copy-editors is also appreciated.

Very many thanks to the families whose candid accounts have made this book possible together with the input from the volunteers from the organisations and the colleagues in schools and other educational organisations. All encounters contributed to the final product and I am truly thankful to every individual who participated in order for me to complete the research.

The thesis from which this book emerged was completed with the assistance of an ESRC studentship. Financial assistance from Darwin College and from an award by the Isaac Newton Trust at the University of Cambridge is also acknowledged, with thanks.

Finally, I acknowledge the 'supreme being' and the many ancestors whose courage and historical legacy have paved the way and provided inspiration and additional motivation at times of particular challenge.

Chapter 1

Introductory insights

The context

'Put 100 people in a room to discuss why black pupils underachieve and watch the arguments start' (Shaw 2003b). A feature of the debate is captured in an article written about an event to discuss Black underachievement: 'teachers blamed parents, parents teachers'. Shaw reports Antoinne pronouncing that 'parents could do more to support their children ... But several mothers said that schools were also to blame, with two saying their children had faced discrimination from white teachers'.

This book seeks to move beyond a culture of blame whilst not shirking some of the more controversial features of this very important albeit somewhat neglected area. Educational policy, practice and research show increased recognition of the role of partnerships between parents and schools in promoting student attainment (DfES 2004a, DfEE 1998, 1991; Devine 2004; Crozier 2000). However, UK African and Caribbean parents, or indeed Black parents in general, are rarely, with notable exceptions (Blair and Bourne 1998; Ellis 1995; Tomlinson 1985; Bryan *et al.* 1985), at the centre of indepth discussions of the home–school relations or parental involvement field. Equally infrequently cited are the associated issues surrounding the proliferation of organisations established specifically to support UK-based African and Caribbean heritage parents in supporting their children through school-aged education and with home–school interaction. These are found from Leeds to London, from Brixton to Bristol. (See Vincent 2000; Hylton 1999; Wright, Weekes and McClaughlin 2000; Reay and Mirza 1997; Crozier 1996.)

The UK research agenda has, to a much greater extent, centred on exploring the 'underachievement' of African and Caribbean (and Bangladeshi and Pakistani) children. Such research is of course important and has gleaned some useful insights (DfES 2004a, 2003; Gillborn and Mirza, 2000; Runnymede Trust 1997; Gillborn and Gipps 1996). However, given the policy and research interest in the role of parental involvement in supporting educational attainment, there is a distinct need for a UK-based study concerned with 'supporting Black pupils through supporting Black parents'. 'Black' in this book refers to families of African and Caribbean heritage.

A review of the literature reinforces Young's view, written in the US, that 'much of the empirical research on best practices within the area of parental involvement has been based on the experiences of middle-class Whites: White middle-class teachers, administrators, support staff, families, and in most instances, White middle-class researchers' (1999: 681). As a member of the Black community in the UK, where African Caribbean researchers such as Mirza (2000), Callender (1997) and Williams (1995) have made similar pronouncements, it seems important to use the insights gained from my Jamaican rooted cultural background and community and professional experience to contribute to this research agenda.

Another part of the rationale for writing this book arises from insights gained from the somewhat uncommon blend of professional and cultural experience of the writer. A prevailing viewpoint among teachers with whom I have worked, at various stages from a classroom teacher to senior manager and education adviser, is that Black parents in general are 'hard to reach' or 'uninvolved' in their children's schooling. The juxtaposition of professional experience in schools and Local Education Authorities (LEAs) and work with Black families in Saturday supplementary schools and other community organisations over several decades suggests a rather more complex picture. When this rather unusual practitioner and community experience is combined with in-depth research, the picture revealed explains some of the reasons why some African and Caribbean families might *appear* to be 'uninvolved' with schools yet, paradoxically, shows how deeply committed they are to supporting their children's educational attainment.

Some issues

One of the most significant questions emerging from this book is the extent to which 'a parent is a parent is a parent' as suggested by a member of one of the parent support organisations. In this viewpoint, Black parents share some of the generic features of home–school relations such as the 'partnership' issues researched comprehensively by writers such as Vincent (1996) and Crozier (2000) in the UK, and Epstein (1992) and Lareau (1989) in the US. The book portrays powerfully some additional issues specific to Black parents, including the impact of institutional racism and cultural stereotyping that Black families have encountered, and with which the organisations, in their different ways, seek to offer support.

In unravelling the circumstances that lead to the need for organisational support, the book provides vivid accounts of the current nature of home–school relations for these families. The compelling portrayals from the empirical evidence enable the reader to understand the needs and expectations of the parents and children studied and the extent to which these relate to the needs and expectations of the children's schools.

Hotly debated issues emerge. These include the impact of race versus social class on home–school interactions and tensions within avowals of partnership and professionalism. Interesting manifestations of power are portrayed. As well as the well-reported situation about the exclusion of Black boys, some of the more intriguing findings from the research surround Black girls who display what the school considers as 'powerful' characteristics and how the exclusion of pupils is often paralleled by the exclusion and marginalisation of their parents. Somewhat unexpectedly, considering the focus on supporting Black pupils by supporting Black parents, parents with children of mixed cultural heritage featured quite strongly in requests for support in home–school interactions.

Through undertaking the study of five organisational approaches to supporting Black parents, we gain understanding of the nature and extent of the organisations' success in meeting the concerns that the parents bring to them in support of their children's school experiences. It leads to increased understanding of the factors behind the current pattern of schooling experienced by the pupils and the parent–school interactions that have led to the involvement of the parents in the different methods of parental support. Some of the organisational support is for and by Black parents, other support is by organisations acting on behalf of Black parents, and further support is organised by Local Education Authorities and schools.

The focus

In investigating these, the specific focus is being made clear. When referring to the parent support organisations' perspectives and more especially those of the parents, it is not African and Caribbean parents in general who are being focused on, it is *those who are interacting with the organisations*. The writer does not intend to extrapolate and generalise empirically from this very distinctive sample of parents to African and Caribbean parents in general. Instead, it is intended to use the findings to develop greater professional understanding, informed by 'culturally convincing' theoretical insights. Practitioners and policy makers at all stages of the education process including teachers, members of school Senior Leadership teams, lecturers, researchers and LEA officers should glean enhanced understanding and information for their work. Members of organisations interested in developing their partnership with parents and schools, particularly Black parents, would certainly benefit. Equally, the case studies of the parents offer a 'real-life' dimension of more general appeal to persons interested in the questions and issues raised by the parents in the case studies; for example, the father who pleads: 'when education fails us and society fails us … when our parents fail us because they don't understand what's happening, where do we turn?' (p. 70).

In selecting the sample of Black parents' support organisations that some parents have turned to, I was interested in cases which appeared to possess a range of different (although not necessarily totally distinct) characteristics in the nature of their interpretation of support to African and Caribbean families, for example advocacy or mediation. Factors such as how long the organisations had been in existence, ownership, the gender and racial characteristics of the personnel were taken into account. Using a combination of knowledge gleaned from informal and formal professional and community-based 'contacts' together with the organisations' own terminology as described by their staff and literature, four cases were selected. The nature of the support on offer was broadly named as advocacy, mediation, home–school liaison, and cultural. They were termed Advocaid, Mediaid, Linkaid and Culturaid. A fifth is a community-based group arising from research opportunities afforded during the study and was called Actionaid to suggest its researcher-initiated action-research origin and connotations of grass-roots action.

The research strategy

The general research strategy was to access the parents and the schools the children attended through information obtained from the organisations. The intention was to gather in-depth responses from key members and families about motives behind the setting up of the organisation and how this fitted into *their* understanding and interpretation of the most appropriate way to proceed in providing support to the families. This approach allows one to meet parents, and in some instances pupils, through the organisations, and gain their perspective of the type of intervention sought by them, together with their understanding of the situation that has led to them becoming involved with the organisations.

In general terms, I used a combination of semi-structured interviews with a selection of parents and staff of the organisations, observations of key meetings, and analysis of a range of documents such as letters to and from the organisations, families and schools. To provide coherence within different research opportunities available at the organisations, a set of core data was required of all support organisations and parents. For organisations, these were their aims, support strategies, why they focused on supporting Black parents, and demographic data about the number and variety of the parents and cases they supported. From all parents, the key data to be gathered were the reason for contact with organisation, the experience of support offered, demographic information about themselves and their child, including race/ethnicity, and their relationship with the school prior to contact with the organisation. The above approach helps to provide focus yet flexibility, for example in interviews. More importantly, it allows one to hear, loud and clear, the voices of the parents, some pupils, and members of the organisations set up to support them.

An overview of the chapters

The book is divided into nine chapters. The first chapter provides a context and rationale to the rising presence of Black parents' support organisations. Associated with this are the personal and professional concerns leading to the study on which the book is raised. Chapter 2 highlights the concerns of Black parents over the decades from their mass arrival in the UK in the 1950s to beyond the new millennium. Key issues and concerns in research, literature and theorisation are debated, setting the scene in the five subsequent chapters (3 to 7) for in-depth studies of five organisations.

The case studies include detailed accounts of families being supported by the organisations, the reasons they are involved, and the organisations' rationale for the type of support being offered. All five offer important insights. Chapter 3 however, which is the first of the case studies, is intentionally the longest. This is to give full justice to the compelling picture of the state of affairs from the 'chalk-face' to the home, gained from direct experience as a home–school liaison teacher (Linkaid) in two schools, resulting in fascinating findings from the action-research opportunities within the role. Chapter 4 highlights what parents at Actionaid, the community organisations, suggest they 'need to know' to support their children's schooling. In Chapter 5, Mediaid portrays the 'let us talk' stance to home–school relations followed in Chapter 6 by the less 'softly softly' position of Advocaid in supporting parents whose children are involved in the school exclusion process. In the final case study, presented in Chapter 7, a group of Black parents support their children's school in 'raising cultural awareness'.

Chapter 8 provides a highly stimulating review of the key issues arising across the case studies, with insights from theory to develop our professional and practitioner understanding and move toward some conclusions. The chapter includes reflections on the methodological process on which the conclusions are based and through which we are able to appreciate what has worked and indeed what has not worked in home–school relations and the depicted organisational support of the parents. Chapter 9, the final chapter, moves from some conclusions toward some solutions in the challenge of progressing toward cultural co-operation rather than cultural exclusion between home, school, and African and Caribbean communities. The different possibilities and limitations of the various means of organisational support for and with these families is recognised whilst showing the potential for the various approaches under particular contexts. The chapter provides 'culturally credible' suggestions for improving the support that schools can offer in supporting Black pupils by supporting Black parents, together with significant implications for policy.

Chapter 2

A parent is a parent is a parent?

The question posed above is key to the issues within this book. As a 'reflective practitioner' questions about the best means of meeting the needs of all families permeated my professional practice. There were also questions about how the race and ethnicity of parents affect the relationship between families and schools.

As a context, it is useful here to remind readers of some historical precursors. While Fryer's *Staying Power: The History of Black People in Britain* (1984) points to a Black presence in Britain centuries before the arrival of the *Empire Windrush* in 1948, the appearance of this ship on the shores of Britain was symbolic of the visibility of groups of African and Caribbean people entering Britain, generally at the expressed invitation of the British Government at the time, who needed their labour. The *Empire Windrush* was one of the first ships on which many of them travelled. Among those on board were the grandparents and parents whose descendants have children currently attending Britain's schools. The multi-faceted areas of the socio-economic disadvantage they encountered on their arrival have been well documented (Smith 1977; Nehaul 1996; Bryan *et al.* 1985). Their socio-economic adversity was often combined with racial hostility against their presence yet they continued to focus their attention on the education of their children. John, a Black educationist, has described the contrast between their previous norms of education and their new encounters:

> Their educational aspirations for their children were matched by an educational culture which induced high self esteem and in which high levels of educational achievement were seen as the norm. In that educational culture your *potential* was not judged by your gender, your race or your class. ... We came here from such an educational culture and were treated as if our grey matter had been forcibly removed on the way and hurled into the Atlantic.
>
> (John 1999: italics added)

John shows also how, on arrival in the UK, the parents were soon organising themselves into groups to provide mutual support and to consider strategies with the potential for rekindling their previous educational culture with its norms of high levels of educational achievement. John describes how these were sometimes set up in people's 'front rooms', at other times in church halls or other community venues. During the 1950s and 1960s, as more of their children were attending British schools, yet achieving relatively little, so the parents became more disgruntled and simultaneously more active in self-support organisations. A 'Black parents' education movement' developed; one which, as Tomlinson described, 'has taken the form of diverse parents' and community groups, who have acted as pressure groups to campaign for improved education for their children, and have organised supplementary education' (1985: 68). Garrison, who in 1976 was one of the founders of the influential ACER (African Caribbean Education Resource) centre in London, points to supplementary schools being viewed by Black parents as:

> channels to enhance black pupils' education and compensating for the lack of cultural support and miseducation in the schools. These schools were seen as a way to make up the deficit features encountered in mainstream schooling's basic delivery which they felt was responsible for the continuing failure.
>
> (1993: 269)

In 1971 Coard published what may be regarded as a seminal text from an African Caribbean perspective: *How the West Indian Child is Made Educationally Subnormal in the British School System*. This articulated forcefully the anger of African and Caribbean parents over the disproportionate number of their children who were being categorised as ESN (educationally subnormal) or labelled as 'difficult' and suspended due to the effects of racism and cultural stereotyping.

It may be considered that Coard's book, in conjunction with the legacy of the Black power movement of the 1960s and 1970s, not only reflected but provided an impact on the widening of the parental and community concerns that were being addressed. A striking example, from the 1970s, is the aims of a particular meeting of the Chapeltown Parents' Action Group in Leeds, this group being formed by a coalition including the West Indian Afro Brotherhood, the United Caribbean Association and the UHURU arts group, as described by Hylton (1999). A selection of their requirements from a 1973 meeting follows:

- more Black governors who are interested in their own people
- better contact between the headmaster, parents and staff
- improved internal facilities of the school

- attempts must be made to slow down the fast teacher turnover in the school
- more Black teachers
- members of the Black community to be invited to speak to the children to give them more motivation
- facilities and staff for extra teaching for the children in the evening
                                              (Hylton 1999: 2 citing Farrar 1992: 56–57)

The above is illustrative of the many aspects of the parents' concerns. It highlights a view which sees the need for the school working with teachers (including more Black teachers), Black parents, governors and other members of the Black community to effect improvement.

The theme of supplementary education is embodied within a call for extra teaching sessions in the evening. Additional to the above, Hylton informs us that the parents 'were able to quote overtly racist remarks' by the head teacher, including that 'Black pupils have lower foreheads and less cranial capacity than the white pupils'. They were therefore campaigning for his removal (1999: 2). Given this context, it seems especially significant that the parents were not calling for 'more Black governors' per se. The implication is that they wanted those who shared and understood their concerns and would be prepared to act in the interest of the Black community where necessary.

The 1980s: A pivotal decade of protest and policy

If Coard's text was the most influential, written from a Black perspective in the 1970s, perhaps the 1980s equivalent, this time written from a Black *feminist* perspective, was that of Bryan *et al.*, *The Heart of the Race: Black Women's Lives in Britain* (1985). The above may be viewed as 1980s Black feminist scholarship in the field of home–school relations. More recently, 'feminist scholarship', with David (2000) as an influential figure, is embedded within the work of writers such as Reay, with a discernable move away from studies of parental involvement toward those concerned with mothers and education. These studies depict the disadvantages faced by working-class mothers in what David has referred to as 'the gendered nuances of power' (1998: 254) in their interactions with schools, despite being 'passionate' (Reay 1998) about their children's education. A study by West *et al.* (1998) in the special issue of the *British Educational Research Journal* devoted to 'Families and education' reflects this perspective.

Bryan *et al.* in the 1980s described how 'Many a Black mother has had to confront, challenge and counteract the second-class, no hope provision we have been offered' (1985: 59). These included challenges to teachers who 'failed to challenge the playground taunting' (p. 63); teachers' 'low expectations' (p. 67); attitudes of careers officers (p. 68); the 'racist assumptions about the intelligence of [their] children (p. 71) and 'arbitrary and often long term suspensions' (p. 77). The label 'troublemakers' was consequently laid on the parents' attempts to represent their child's interests. The chapter recalls, however, how 'our parents, anxious that we should escape the menial, low paid work they had been forced to accept, urged us to seize any educational opportunity that came our way' (p. 68).

The 1980s, as Tomlinson (1997) argues, formed a critical period in Black education. Consistent with the writing from Bryan et al., she cites the Rampton Committee's interim report highlighting 'a gulf of mistrust and misunderstanding' and also that 'parents had lost faith in schools to make improvements' (Rampton 1981 cited by Tomlinson 1997: p.15). The 'loss of faith' by Black communities was fused by the tensions engendered by that which Black males in particular experienced as unjust police treatment, described in the Scarman report (1981). The most visible image of the 1980s occurred on the streets of urban localities throughout the UK in the form of 'riots', 'urban protest' (Solomos 1986) or 'disorders' (Riley 1994).

The Rampton Report (1981) cited by Tomlinson above and the Swann Report, *Education for All* (1985), were two key educational policy documents with a focus on Black communities. Between them the two reports covered issues of direct bearing to Black parents: underachievement of minority ethnic groups; racism 'both intentional and unintentional' and the role of teacher education in developing diversity in the curriculum; and the recruitment of ethnic minority teachers.

The 1990s and beyond the millennium

Ellis (1995), in her text aimed at Black parents, *Schooling Black children in Britain: a practical guide*, offers a contrast between the parents who arrived earlier and the current perspective.

> The people who came to Britain in the 1950s and 60s had little control over the work they did, even though they did it to the best of their abilities. Today we no longer expect the next generation to continue doing only dirty, unskilled or semi-skilled work which the white population does not wish to do. But in order for our children to gain access to all levels of the British work force, parents and members of the Black community must make it their duty to play an active part in their children's schooling, and make sure they get the skills necessary to take their rightful place in the work force.
>
> (1995: ii)

The above continues themes such as the need for community as well as individual efforts and it is still assumed that the school will not equip their children with the necessary skills. The type of value the parents place on education is implicit in the above, as is the suggestion that Black parents and communities have more control than previously in exercising their parental and community *duty* to ensure that their children are more equipped educationally hence vocationally. Ellis later discusses how, whilst advocating this need, there is awareness that as Black people, their progress may be constrained due to racism and discrimination.

Ellis's text may be contextualised within the literature of the 1990s and the new millennium with a thrust of 'guidance', 'successful strategies' and 'best practice'. Another Black woman writer, Williams, is 'concerned with identifying some of the strategies African Caribbean parents use to prepare young children for a predominantly White Euro centric school environment'. She asks questions such as 'Why is it that some Black children survive school more successfully than others, when race and racism are factors adversely impinging on all Black children? Could parents, home and the community actively contribute to making Black children's school experiences fundamentally different?' (1995: 149–150). In her examination of these questions, Williams, like Bryan *et al.* (1985), points to the role of Black mothers, whom, she affirms, 'have exhibited a fierce dedication to the advancement and education of their children … Sacrifices made to obtain education have traditionally been seen as investments for the future' (154). She reports them using strategies to 'develop a positive sense of self'.

Crozier (1996), writing on 'Black Parents and School Relationships', reports the parents, especially those with primary children, undertaking similar academic activities: 'reading … playing games … mathematics work or helping with spelling' (1996: 256). They were described as 'diligent', which included 'attending parents' evenings, reading their children's reports and making comments on these if asked to do so' (1996: 256). However, two of the five parents with children at secondary school portrayed the 'negative experiences' of their children, and their concerns repeated those discussed in the literature from previous decades: 'Low expectations, and stereotypical views'. For all, 'race is an issue underpinning either their children's education or their experiences as a parent, or both' (1996: 256). The portrayal is of a small group of parents (five African Caribbean, one 'Asian') who use various interventions in support of their children's schooling.

In the first decade of the new millennium, the terminology occasionally changes but many concerns remain. The 'under-representation' of Black children in high-attaining examination statistics and their over-representation in 'arbitrary and long term' exclusions (Smith 1998; Osler 1997; Gillborn 1996, 1995) is debated at conferences such as 'The Education of the Black Child' (2003).

Poignantly, the experience of Doreen Lawrence, together with her husband Neville, is reminiscent of Bryan *et al.*'s contention that 'Like our relationship with the police, education has been a crucial issue for the Black community'

(1985: 58). It was the long-standing grass-roots campaign of these two African and Caribbean parents, Doreen and Neville Lawrence, over police inaction and discriminatory behaviour after the racially motivated murder of their school-aged 'model pupil' son Stephen, that led to the Macpherson Report. The tenacity of their campaign in the face of numerous obstacles by the police, and the grass-roots support that sustained them along the way, may be considered an example of 'fierce dedication' and 'collective struggle'.

The resultant intense media coverage of the inquiry and subsequent report signalled the end of what Gillborn (1995) referred to as a 'deracialised' discourse. The police were deemed to be institutionally racist in their approach to the investigation, especially in the failure to take seriously from the onset the possibility that the murder could have been racially motivated. All the media discussed the implications of 'institutional racism' re-emerging from the context of Stokely Carmichael and the Black Power movement of 1960s America.

> The collective failure of an organisation to provide an appropriate and professional service to people because of their colour, culture or ethnic origin. It can be seen or detected in processes, attitudes and behaviour which amounts to discrimination through unwitting prejudice, ignorance, thoughtlessness and racist stereotyping which disadvantages minority ethnic people.
>
> (Macpherson 1999: 32)

The influence of this report may be seen in the amendment to the Race Relations Act (2000) that makes it a *statutory* duty for public services, including the police force, Local Educational Authorities, schools and hospitals, to operate in a non-discriminatory manner. It covers service provision and recruitment policies including the duty to have in place a Race Equality Policy demonstrating that the service does not discriminate against any groups. As part of their Race Equality Policy, schools are required to record and monitor racist incidents and show that they have proactive strategies to foster racial harmony. Ofsted's framework for inspection of schools from 2003 is clearly cognisant of this Act. In assessing the standards achieved by pupils, inspectors now interpret and report on 'the school's analysis of how different groups of pupils perform ... the relative achievement of boys and girls, and different groups and individuals, especially those from different ethnic backgrounds and those whose home language is not English' (Ofsted 2003: 33).

Key policy developments

The emergence of the more racialised discourse is also exemplified in the range of publications with a specific focus on African and Caribbean communities with explicit attention to issues of race, combating racism and underachievement.

The DfES (2003) consultation document *Aiming High: Raising the Achievement of Minority Ethnic Pupils* after its consultation has separate sections on Parental and Community Involvement, with case study examples of 'what works?' This builds on Blair and Bourne's (1998) contribution to the 'successful strategies' literature. Published during the time of the Stephen Lawrence Inquiry, it contains valuable case study examples of successful practice:

> One school provided space and opportunities for parents of Black children to meet and discuss issues and concerns, which they could take up with staff.
>
> The most effective schools were listening schools, which took time to talk with students and parents, which took seriously the views that students and parents offered and their own interpretation of school processes; and which used this learning to re-appraise and where necessary change, their practices.
>
> (1998: 7)

The above has a stronger and more contemporary 'edge' to the theme of 'partnership' with parents that has dominated policies and literature since the 1960s, although not generally incorporating a perspective on Black parents. To Cullingford, 'partnership implies mutual respect and recognition of the different types of help that children need' (1996: 3). Vincent discussed partnership from a more critical perspective and critiqued the Plowden Report, one of the earliest reports on home–school relations. According to Vincent, 'the goal was to convert as many *individual* parents as possible to supporting the goals of the schools ... [it was] a consensus view of home school relationships ... to include those parents who were co-operative and supportive' (1996: 25). 'Supportive' tends to imply support of the school by parents' involvement in their children's learning activities. This co-operative emphasis on the way in which partnership is framed in policy underlies concepts such as parents as co-educators, while the need for communication and collaboration is embodied in policies such as Home–School Agreement, with an emphasis on shared responsibility. The complexity of putting partnership in practice is a frequent theme within both UK literature (Crozier 2000; Bastiani 1991) and that of the US (Lareau 1989). The titles of Crozier's article 'Parents and Schools: Partnership or Surveillance?' (1998) and her book, *Parents and Schools: Partners or Protagonists?* (2000) portray both the complexity and tensions of home–school relations.

The pursuit of partnership is now being extended to organisations including those of the 'Black Education Movement' to help other sectors to combat social and educational issues. A study by Bastiani into supplementary school provision in the CfBT/Lambeth Education Action Zone highlights their 'strong parental involvement' and a 'family atmosphere' (2000: 133). What Bastiani suggests is *new* is a recognition by others of the potential of these organisations. Implicit in his account is that schools can learn from the parents and community members involved. The DfES supplementary school support has echoed this stance.

An important Runnymede Trust research-based report has highlighted the existence and importance of Black parents' support groups including schools that are actively seeking partnerships with Black parents through setting up school-based support groups.

> There are a multitude of parent support groups and community centres which advocate on the behalf of parents and pupils when a decision to exclude has been made, or where a difficult relationship between the pupil and the school has developed. However, though these services do exist within Black communities, Black parents continue to feel isolated and unaware of where to go for help and advice ... Many schools are now keen to develop Black parent support groups to give parents the opportunity to discuss difficult issues with each other.
>
> (Runnymede Trust 1998: 9)

Three types of groups were illustrated in the above Runnymede Trust report: those external to the school concentrating on advocacy over exclusions; school-based support groups; and a brief case study of 'The Camden Black Parents' and Teachers' Association'. The CBPTA provides a supplementary school alongside advocacy, advice and a support group for parents (Runnymede Trust 1998: 10). These types of organisations, set up to support Black parents both in and out of school, are indicative of those that I will be investigating in this study.

Theoretical insights

Williams, a Black woman in the UK, writes that 'our exclusions and marginalisation from traditional academic discourse resulted not only in our experiences being distorted and excluded, but also in having only limited opportunities within which to formulate "our own" theoretical explanations of our lives' (1995: 150). It is intended that this section will contribute to addressing this noticeable gap in the home–school relations research agenda.

Collins' African American feminist insights, while not fully transferable to the UK given their different socio-cultural histories, also offers an important historical basis for theory development in this area. She points out 'the centrality of Black women as everyday political activists' and argues that 'This overall philosophy of education as a group effort has its roots in the slave experience' (1996: 148).

It is no accident that many well-known Black women activists were either teachers or somehow involved in struggling for educational opportunities for African-Caribbeans of both sexes ... Educated Black women were brought up to see their education as something gained not just for their own development but for the purpose of race uplift. This feeling was so strong that the women founding the National Association of Coloured Women's clubs chose as their motto 'Lifting as we Climb'.

(1996: 149)

Although this is within a Black American context, the concept of 'race uplift' and 'collectives' in this process would seem to have some resonance in the historical tradition of the 'Black Education Movement' in Britain. Certainly, Bryan *et al.*, when writing in 1985, while not using the term 'race uplift', did seem to consider that education required a community-wide response. Likewise, the subtitle of their chapter 'Learning to resist' has intriguing connotations of learning as a form of resistance to the cultural stereotypes being propounded. It is also reminiscent, as Collins and others have reminded us, that within the slavery experience, the act of learning to read and write as a step toward becoming educated was one of subversion since it was punishable by death, yet such acts continued.

A theorisation of collective resistance by Black parents and children as a form of resistance to structural inequalities across and within institutions has been offered by several researchers, e.g. Hylton (1999) and Gilroy (1987). Mac an Ghaill (1988) cites Gilroy:

Localised struggle over education, racist violence and police practices continually reveal how Blacks have made use of notions of the community to organise themselves. Involvement in local community politics provided an insight into theorising the different forms of resistance to racism and authoritarianism within schools, as linked to their parents' survival strategies. They made clear their understanding of their children's critical response to school, as part of their resistance to racism.

(1988: 163)

The potential power of the organisations and potential agency or 'parent power' in making use of the organisations necessitates reference to the relationship between agency and structure. In an insightful section on 'agency and structure considered' McNamara *et al.* provide an overview of what is referred to as 'agency/structure dilemmas' in the specific field of home–school relations (2000: 475–477). It is not the intention here to address fully this theoretical debate. I will focus on the nature and extent to which the activities of the organisations enable them to exert power, or to which the parents exert agency in taking an active stance to fulfil their goal of supporting Black children through their schooling experiences. It includes developing understanding of constraints on their action by structural societal inequalities within a consideration of agency and structure.

Giroux has suggested that 'educational theory and practice stands at an impasse ... a strongly embedded dualism which separates human agency and structural analysis' (1983: 119). Giddens work, however, indicates that this might be overstating the case for duality (1994).

In attempting to formulate theoretical explanations, the traditional process is through building on those currently available within the academy. Given that within academia, the distinctive realities and experiences of Black communities have been largely neglected, one useful contribution of this study is to use the specific realities and experiences which arise from the study to consider the extent to which the existing theories may be relevant and to either develop them or suggest alternative theoretical explanations.

Hall, one of the founders of cultural criticism, accomplished both over the time of his eminent academic career. Mercer has argued that in Hall's 'neo-Gramscian approach to the problem of structure and agency ... relations of power and resistance enter representations and consciousness unevenly' (Mercer 2000: 238). In an article published during the critical mid-1980s period, Hall discussed 'Gramsci's relevance for the study of race and ethnicity' (1986). A Gramscian conceptualisation of hegemony in particular may provide some insights for this study. 'Hegemony' refers to the ways in which dominant groups are said to maintain their power over subordinates not by forceful means, but by the 'ensemble of relations – the complex of activities, beliefs and norms deeply embedded in civil society, in everyday life' (1971: 210). In this type of theorisation, the beliefs and values that schools, the media and other cultural forms of expression portray as attributes of good parents and their depiction of the role of parents in relation to professionals may provide some schools with justification for their institutional practices. When summarised, as is necessary here, Gramsci's theories may appear deterministic. They were, however, developed as premises for political struggle. Individual and collective resistance to some of these processes amidst the consent of many was part of the way in which the process operated unevenly as Mercer referred to above and Hall was able to extrapolate from Gramsci's theories. It is this aspect of theorisation that may have applicability here.

Relevant also for this exploration is the term 'Structure Versus Culture' coined by McCarthy (1998: 54), a Black academic writing in the US. In undertaking such an exploration, I make explicit that the theoretical approach to be adopted is intended to address the 'real world' nature of the task. The organisations and families are to be theoretically construed as neither victims of 'cultural collision' in relation to the power of the school nor, conversely, champions of cultural agency overcoming all structural barriers.

Culture and cultural capital

The approach to a definition of culture which I am applying for the purposes of this study is that employed by Spradley (1979). The following two extracts adopt a cultural perspective, which implicitly reveals Spradley's anthropological roots.

> Culture refers to the acquired knowledge that people use to interpret experience and generate social behaviour ... Culture, as a shared system of meanings, is learned, revised, maintained, and defined, in the context of people interacting
>
> (Spradley 1979: 6)

What is attractive about Spradley's definition for this study is that it avoids a prescriptive, essentialist tone. Later, he likens culture to a 'map [which] serves as a guide for acting and for interpreting our experience; it does not compel us to follow a particular course' (1975: 7). Additionally, he quotes Frake, stating, 'People are not just map readers, they are map makers ... culture does not provide a cognitive map, but rather a set of principles for map making and navigation'. As a researcher, one can attempt to gain important cultural insights about particular groups without extending this to the adoption of a definitive representation, which would imply, for example, that *all* working-class people or even all black working-class boys or girls essentially behave in a particular way. It avoids what Spradley has termed the 'ethnocentrism' of aspects of the western research tradition.

Likewise, the term 'Black communities' has been used intentionally. One is not suggesting that there is a homogenous 'Black Community' or even homogenous 'African Caribbean or Caribbean Communities' any more than a white community, with homogenous values and attitudes. One of the means of expressing agency, perhaps based on a historical necessity, which many people with African and Caribbean ancestry have adopted at various historical points and locations, is grouping together for a specific purpose or common goal. In practical terms, as Gilroy (1987) above, Chevannes and Reeves (1987) and Tomlinson (1985), for example, have portrayed, African and Caribbean communities have been among groups, including some 'Asian' and especially Muslim families, who have organised themselves to exert such community agency in relation to education, as white socialist groups have in earlier times.

The above theorisation, when linked with Bourdieu's (1986a) concept of 'cultural capital', provides potentially a helpful theoretical lens through which to view aspects of this study. In Bourdieu's theorisation, schools, as institutions, can transform resources from a particular 'habitus' – i.e. way of thinking, behaviour and attitudes – into 'capital' to draw education and wider social and material benefits for those sharing the same cultural values.

The possession of cultural resources in the same currency as required by the culture of the school is theoretically construed as accruing benefits which can be reinvested for the next generation, thereby resulting in a form of cultural reproduction. Conversely, those families with cultural resources not valued by the school are devalued and disadvantaged. Lareau (1989) in the US has referred to a 'home advantage' for upper middle-class parents. Researchers such as Reay (1998) have used this as a basis of a class analysis of (predominantly white) mothers in the field of home–school interactions, where she asserts that despite the 'hard labour' of mothering shared by both middle-class and working-class parents, middle-class mothers are 'able to make the education system work for them' in the way that working-class mothers are unable to' (1998: 197).

If one very tentatively takes the academic licence to extend this aspect of Bourdieu's theories to encompass the dimension of race, the possibilities are that minority ethnic communities may be perceived by institutions to be without such cultural resources. The parents' culture may also be viewed in this way, so that the African and Caribbean parents, like the white working-class parents, may start from a position of disadvantage in relation to the school.

The significance or otherwise of social class as applied to Black families whose children attend state schools would need to be addressed in the light of the findings from Gillborn and Mirza (2000) revealing that social class for Black parents did not have the amount of impact for children in relation to education outcomes as for some other groups. Moore, a Black HMI, in a conference presentation (1999) referred to the phenomenon of Black children starting their schooling off, from home, at an apparent academic advantage and leaving as some of the most disadvantaged academically, which was later reported in Gillborn and Mirza's study. Moore posed the question: What happens to them at school?

Both ethnic differences and the effects of racism need to be considered in addition to a class analysis in order to appreciate the effects of material disadvantages and the impact of cultural experiences. In exploring these issues, it may be important to distinguish between Black in general and being African or Caribbean in particular. In considering home–school relations for African and Caribbean families in Britain and support for them in supporting their children's schooling, it seems timely to investigate the role of organisations established to support these parents' support of their children in schooling issues and to uncover practice and formulate theories that may assist our understanding of some of these issues. It is to this we now turn.

We will start with Linkaid, as it contains detailed accounts from parents and pupils, based on 'hands on' experience in a home–school liaison role.

Chapter 3

Linkaid: 'You're here for the school'

An LEA home–school liaison role

Home–school liaison: salient features

Linkaid is LEA-inspired support in the form of home–school liaison. Home–school liaison is generally set up by an LEA or school with the intention of forging an alliance between the school and parents which is intended for all parties to work together to help meet the interests of the child, particularly in relation to raising achievement. It is considered as a preventative strategy aimed largely at pupils at risk of underachievement. Promoting pupil achievement and 'the active involvement of African Caribbean parents' were two core areas of my responsibility whilst employed in the position of home–school liaison for the Multicultural Education Service (hereafter referred to as MES) of an LEA, one day a week. The role required two terms at Actdale school followed by two terms at Actmount school.

'We work in partnership with schools and parents', said Linkaid's mission statement. In this chapter, I illustrate the extent to which schools worked in partnership with parents. I then present some key issues arising from the action research opportunities within the home–school liaison role.

The two schools I was allocated to 'work in partnership' contained the highest proportion of African and Caribbean students in the LEA. The following letter from a head teacher to Miranda, the Linkaid area manager, was found to be characteristic of the type of input schools sought.

> I have now been able to consult with my colleagues with regard to target areas for African Caribbean pupils.
>
> In general terms we would like an initial focus on individual pupils to raise their achievement in specific areas of the curriculum, also leading to an opportunity to gain their perspective of the school in order to develop strategies for the pupils.

Support to pupils and their families: case studies

As above, schools tended to request, in the first instance, a 'focus on individual pupils'. Four pupils, Chamberlain and Clark in school one, Actdale; and Wambu and Brewster in school two, Actmount, were selected from a list provided by the school. For ease of reference I have included only the child's surname, with the parent being called Mr or M(r)s. Hence, Chamberlain is the first young person and his parents will be referred to as Mr and Mrs Chamberlain. The families were selected on the basis that regular contact with them was part of the Linkaid support *and* that the parents had become involved with Actionaid and would therefore be able to offer a perspective on both.

School one: Actdale

Chamberlain and his family

'We told them from day one'

Where parents reported problems with the school, they tended to be described as starting quite soon after the child's entry. In the case of Mrs Chamberlain, it was 'from day one'.

> We told them right from day one that Chamberlain was very bright, very intelligent and unless they challenged him intellectually they would have problems with him. The first day we went for the interview with Mrs Wilson [Head of Year]. Chamberlain was very angry. We'd just moved back from the States and he didn't want to come home. We tried to explain to her, we took all his school records and everything. She didn't even wanna look at those.
>
> [Researcher: And what did the school records say?]
>
> That he was a straight 'A' student and he was in the gifted class programme in the States, which meant one day a week he went off to another school with a busload of kids and they would be taught a couple of years ahead of their age, and she didn't wanna know, she didn't even look at his records.

'Didn't wanna know'

The frustration of Mrs Chamberlain is noticeable in the repetition of phrases about the Head of Year not prepared to even 'look at' the evidence of her son's intelligence she and her husband had brought in the form of his academic records. Her first impression was that the teacher 'didn't wanna know' about her child's ability.

The above account helped to contextualise the reaction I had previously received from the same teacher, Mrs Wilson, Chamberlain's current Head of Year. In none of my interaction with her did she mention Chamberlain's intellectual aptitude. Early on in the post, I had asked for information from her Head of Year position about those students on the list I had been given to work with. She had excused herself from a pre-arranged meeting with a note stating: 'Sorry I can't meet you today. I have had a chat with Jane [Linkaid school contact]. Perhaps you could talk with her.'

Attempting to meet the needs of Chamberlain, his family and school

'He's bright, could get excellent exam results but doesn't know when to keep his mouth shut', was the comment made by Jane, the school's Linkaid team leader, at the briefing session where she provided the list of pupils she wanted me to work with.

Repeated interactions with the family over the two terms at the school enabled me to establish that critical episodes with *particular teachers* had negatively impacted on home–school relations. Only one occurred whilst I was Linkaid teacher. According to Mrs Chamberlain:

> We caught too many of the teachers doing things that if they were in the workplace they could possibly get fired for but because children are involved they don't seem to get any protection against those things. Although I know that he's possibly fifty or seventy per cent responsible for suspensions and whatnot because he's argumentative I also know that teachers have been in the wrong as well but the school has never acknowledged that and I think that's wrong. That means my child has no protection in that school and when I actually said that to the principal he turned round and said to me condescendingly, 'Mrs Chamberlain, I am a parent too'.

'My child has no protection'

As a parent, she believed that 'the school expects support in trying to get their job done but it's very hard to give support if your child is unhappy there and you don't feel they're supporting the child'. Support, in her view, was a two-way process. She would support the school over her child's 'argumentative' manner: she also wanted the school to support *her* over her son if a teacher had been 'in the wrong'. In this situation, her repeat of the word 'protection' seemed indicative of its importance to her. This was contrasted with her views about herself, 'I don't care how they treat me as a parent. I just want them to treat my child right and be fair'.

I know Chamberlain is a handful and I understand how a teacher can be frustrated and how hard it must be and I've always gone to the school and stood up for the school if he's been rude to a teacher or whatever. I've always supported the school if Chamberlain's behaviour has been in the wrong. But my argument is that a lot of teachers shouldn't be in the school if they can't be professional and if they can't be unbiased and if they can't give the child a second chance.

Mrs Chamberlain's expectations of teachers as 'professional' are embodied in characteristics of being 'unbiased' and 'giving 'a second chance'. As the above illustrates, her expectations were not being met.

From the school's perspective, Chamberlain was indeed considered 'a handful' and *their* expectations were not being met. I soon discovered that his behaviour was a general concern to teachers; even those who had never taught him. As one such teacher explained: 'I don't *teach* him but I've had some run-ins. He was going to school, I asked him to get off his bike. He did get off but not without being completely rude and offensive.' On being asked to explain this, her response was, 'It was his manner and attitude. I get the impression he doesn't respect members of staff. I had a word and told his form teacher.'

The word 'respect' also arose from Mrs Chamberlain. 'He's not going to respect them just because they're teachers. He feels it's to be earned with intelligence and ability to teach. He feels that the teachers here do not teach.' Chamberlain's reason for citing one teacher whom he respected was that:

> She was more bothered about whether people learnt and whether they had a good productive lesson than whether you were doing exactly what you were supposed to be doing, like whether you were talking, she basically made everyone responsible for their own learning.

'More focused on schooling than they are on discipline'

The features of this teacher's style seemed similar to the schooling Chamberlain had experienced in America. In general, he and his family compared his American experience of schooling more favourably:

> In America, they are a lot more individual, they allow you to be what you want to be, the schools over here, you've got to do this, do that, you have to be back from lunch by a certain time and if you're late you get detentions. In America, they are more focused on schooling than they are on discipline.

The significance of the phrase 'more focused on schooling than they are on discipline' was also key to Mrs Chamberlain's concern. 'I tried to explain if you don't keep him challenged and keep him in the top set you'll get trouble. But they were telling me he can't go into top sets until his behaviour improved.' When compared with the views of Chamberlain's mother, this seemed to reflect *both* their desires: teachers that were 'more focused on schooling than ... on discipline'.

'A go ahead, open type of person'

A senior manager at the school, who had recently been appointed to the forthcoming head teacher's position was singled out for praise and respect by Mrs Chamberlain, on the basis that:

> I don't feel for one moment she's racist but I also think she's a go ahead, open type of person ... and then when there was an occasion when Chamberlain was right she stood up for him ... I think she will do a lot for the different cultures in the school.

She reported, however, that 'Chamberlain would have gone by then, it'll be too late for him'.

It was not 'too late' according to the results of classroom observations and the teachers I spoke to in connection with the targets for individual support of the students. Chamberlain was submitting more coursework. However, monitoring of attendance noted a change in attendance pattern as well as an alteration in attitude. In an earlier home-based interview with the family, Chamberlain had compared himself with his friend Craig, another person on the list, who was a repeated truant: 'I'm still going to school even though the teachers are treating me like shit.' What Chamberlain called the 'straw that broke the camel's back', concerned an incident where a teacher 'made a racist statement' to him, after seeing him with a hat and Mr 'X' (the head teacher) had 'still not done anything', as Chamberlain described in an interview after he had left.

'I went through all the right channels'

> I just refused to go into school any more. Because for years they were saying to me, look, if you're done wrong by a teacher don't say anything, accept it and go and tell the principal, so I took it, I went and told the principal. This was basically the straw that broke the camel's back because at the end of the day there was always that little piece of hope that they would be on my side. I was so angry I just didn't bring myself to do anything foolish. I went through all the right channels, I did everything right and I ended up getting suspended so I just refused to go.

For Chamberlain's mother, whilst the above undoubtedly had an impact, it was another incident that most concerned her. During an interview, Mrs Chamberlain was clearly upset at a reference that the Head of Year had sent to a prestigious sixth form college that Chamberlain was hoping to attend. Describing the Head of Year as a 'prize bitch and a racist' she asserted: 'The reference was very spiteful. She's spiteful; she has a prejudice against Chamberlain as a person. She *made* him sign it then she wrote the stuff in it and sent it to other teachers.' Chamberlain agreed that when he had signed his portion it was blank. Mrs Chamberlain, however, informed me that she had refused to sign her section when she saw what the Head of Year had written. I was provided with a copy, which reflected her comments on its content.

Attempts to support

Attempting to support the family with their concerns over individual teachers proved the most problematic aspect of the home–school liaison Linkaid role. A senior manager's response concerning the member of staff who had triggered Chamberlain's 'last straw' was that 'he's like that with everyone, that's just his way'. When I had an opportunity to interview some white parents from a local group, some of whom had actually been pupils at the school, the same teacher's name came up as 'horrible, he was so *rude*'. From the perspective of the Chamberlain family, however, 'racism' was added to his rudeness. The effect, from the father's report, was that 'the teacher didn't get a reprimand for calling him racial (sic) names and then Chamberlain's behaviour just went downhill'.

The family seemed to appreciate that I listened to their concerns and that I was prepared to approach the school. Mrs Chamberlain, however, was very clear that 'there's no point, he's leaving soon, you keep out of it or you won't be able to help other parents. Help him know what he's supposed to do so he can get through his exams, that's the most important thing'. She then wrote a letter to the school herself.

Chamberlain's mother's wish coincided with Chamberlain's own desire to learn and pass his exams. Although I had noted that he had 'refused' to go back to school, despite concerted efforts, I continued to monitor the progress of his work, consulting with teachers, whilst he was on 'study leave'. This seemed to be working as a strategy as he was concentrating on completing his coursework and was, according to most of his teachers, 'on target'. Although Chamberlain was not attending, he was, in effect, 'responsible for [his] own learning'. He submitted his coursework on time, revised at home, turned up for exams and obtained seven GCSEs at grades C and above; although not all the 'A' and 'B' grades that his former academic record would suggest that he was capable of. He then went to college and took 'A' levels, which I understand he found 'much better than at school'.

The Clark family

'They should inform me'

The intervention with the Clark family at Actdale school was due to the son, a year younger than Chamberlain and in the first year of his two-year GCSE course. His mother, in an interview, reported a lack of information about his academic progress, as indicated in the following response to a question about expectations of the school:

> I think that there should be more progress reports. You don't know what your child is doing, bad or good, unless you go to a parents' evening and that can be too late. I think that if your child is under-achieving then they should inform me. They let you know when your child has been rude but not when your child is underachieving, especially Black children.

'You do need to push your child more'

The key concern of Mrs Clark was indeed her son's achievement. The reasons for this were explained in response to a question about whether she thought there were things related to Black parents that were different for white parents in supporting their child:

> Yes I do. It's so much harder for the Black child to go out in the wide world and be successful than it is for a white person. You do need to push your child more and you need to be on top of them more because it is so much harder.

The difficulty of job prospects for Black persons in relation to white persons was one of the reasons for 'pushing' her son:

> Where a white person can go and get a job, you've got to have three times the amount of qualifications for you to even get to that position. That's why you've got to push the child that much harder. As much as they might see it as nagging, it's not nagging. It's for their own good, they will look back.

Distinguishing 'pushing' from nagging was important to Mrs Clark, as indicated by the way in which she mentioned this on at least two other occasions.

Supporting the Clark family

I supported Mrs Clark by assisting her in her efforts to 'push' her son. As part of this process I became the bearer of informal progress reports through asking several subject teachers to provide information about his progress. On the whole, their comments about Clark were very different from those about Chamberlain. A representative statement was: 'Oh he's lovely, a very amiable boy. He can be a bit silly though. He enjoys the subject. He's a team player and very confident.'

An exception to the teachers' focus on his 'amiability' was Jane, the school-based Linkaid team leader who had placed the names on the list. Her concentration on his academic progress was consistent with Mrs Clark's view of her.

> She is one of the best teachers there that I can say has influenced me and helped me to sort of look at certain situations.
>
> [Researcher: Situations ... like what?]
>
> Well, like Clark's work on the whole, certain things that you would sort of sit back and not really think about. The way she speaks you sort of think to yourself well, I really do need to check out my child and see how well my child is doing, and things like where she thinks that my child has done good, she will say 'right let's push them to get him up into another group' going that stage further, she's there and she does really strike a backbone and she does really stand behind you when you're trying to get the best for your child.

The terminology of 'pushing' was repeated by Mrs Clark throughout our interactions. As above, it included noting those teachers who, like Jane, 'pushed' her child academically, acting as a 'backbone' to support her own efforts. According to Jane, our Linkaid role was to support parents and the school as part of the pushing process. Her estimation of his academic ability seemed to concur with Mrs Clark's own view, expressed to me informally, that 'I know he's not academically minded, he'll never gets As or Bs, but he could, if pushed, get Cs'. In order to support him in this, Mrs Clark mainly used her own efforts, and spoke with teachers herself, only enlisting my support, knowledge and contact with the teachers at the school to prompt teachers who had not responded. She also discussed with me the pros and cons of the school suggesting that her son moves up a group in Maths. She 'wasn't sure', she said, 'because he may have to be with the teacher he was with before, that he had a lot of trouble with'. Her son had said that he would 'prefer not to'. She described her son as having a 'personality clash' with a couple of teachers, one of whom was the person who would be teaching him if he moved to another group.

More direct support was called upon only once. It was from the Head of Department that Mrs Clark had asked for a meeting with concerning her child's progress in the class of one of his team. The Head of Department asked me to 'come along' saying 'I know you've been working with the mother'. Mrs Clark had already discussed the meeting with me and also wanted me to attend. In the meeting, Mrs Clark took the lead in explaining the situation, with one or two requests for points of clarification by me. Both agreed a course of action and both seemed satisfied with the outcome. Privately, the Head of Department pointed out that the teacher concerned was 'quite new to the profession'. Privately, Mrs Clark suggested that the teacher was 'feisty'. No subsequent problems with the teacher took place as far as I was aware. Notwithstanding the above situation, Mrs Clark's relationship with the school in general was, she said, 'Not too bad'.

> On the whole I don't get any complaints about Clark. He gets on with most of the teachers. He seems to be a well-behaved child. I have had a few problems. I've had someone on the phone to say he has done something. Clark has always admitted his mistakes. He will accept the punishment or whatever. It's like fights and things like that. And some of it has been racist, most of the time it's because children have been racist towards him so he will lash out.

While at the school I did not receive any complaint about Clark's behaviour or work, aside from the one teacher, described above. There was no occasion when Clark was involved in a fight. In response to Mrs Clark's comment about this, however, I asked her about the kind of advice she offered her son and what the school's response had been. Her reply had echoes of the Chamberlain family. 'They always say tell the teachers but people get very disheartened because they do take it to the teacher and nothing is done about it.' She represented the situation from her child's viewpoint: 'If you're not seeing anything being done about it what is the point of taking it to the teacher whereas if you give them a good thump, you would feel a lot happier than seeing it go by.'

As a mother, however, she asserted: 'I think you should go to the proper channels.' This, she explained, meant:

> Take it to the teacher and then keep on to make sure something is done to reprimand the child for their actions. I don't think they should get away with any racism or bullying or anything like that. The teachers will say, 'oh ignore them' but it's not them that has been offended.

Her use of 'the proper channels', the same phrase used by Chamberlain, was noted. The above suggesting that, although it was a child rather than a teacher who was the cause of her concern, Mrs Clark may not have been satisfied with the school's initial response and had to 'keep on to make sure something [was done] to reprimand the child'. This seemed similar to her views and actions regarding the progress of her child, to 'get something done' there was a need to 'keep on'.

An achievement session: 'Start of a good thing'

As well as working with individual pupils and their parents, it was necessary to provide specific whole-school strategies to raise achievement. The best approach, I decided, was to incorporate any such strategy within the existing structures of the school. I therefore organised an achievement evening by incorporating the target of 'establishing a clear understanding of the role of parents, school and child' within associated goals of the school development plan. The achievement evening was designed for parents of African and Caribbean children and their child, with a special, but not exclusive targeting of those parents with children in years 10 and 11. The invitation highlighted the informal and social nature of the occasion and that university students would be present as they were keen to act as 'linkpersons' with the students. The invitation was widely accepted.

From the feedback from parents and staff and analysis of a video recording of the event, the session was successful on a number of levels. A senior manager and other teachers and LEA staff who unexpectedly appeared as 'observers' commented that I was able to attract a range of different parents, some of whom had rarely attended school functions. Both Mrs Chamberlain and Mrs Clark attended. It was a considerable time later that I discovered that at least two of the parents and their children had extremely negative attitudes toward the school and some of its teachers.

There were also more subtle features of success. I had, for example, managed to enlist the support of some parents in organising the event in ways they felt comfortable. Some came early to help to prepare the room with material they had provided, the cooking of the Caribbean food was shared between the parents and myself, parents elected a parent from each group to discuss the result of their workshop activity with the rest, and parent notetakers were appointed for the feedback. What was evident from observations of the discussion was that the parents were pleased with the opportunity of sharing their views. The result: their written feedback begins with the words 'start of a good thing' and ends with 'we need more meetings like this'. In between were matters like 'not informed early of underachievement'.

To keep the momentum, the event was placed as an agenda item at the next Linkaid school team meeting closely followed by a meeting with the head teacher, who was also provided with a written summary for the senior leadership team (SLT). To maximise its impact, the feedback and suggestions from the parents' achievement session were supplemented with extracts from an Ofsted report on *Raising the Attainment of Minority Ethnic Pupils* (Ofsted 1999). Judicious selections included ethnic monitoring; the effects of cultural stereotyping; the need for a whole-school approach led by the SLT; and making effective use of EMAG (Ethnic Minority Assessment Grant) funded staff, parents and the local community to address the achievement of Black students.

Soon after the above, the member of senior leadership with oversight of Linkaid discussed with me a proposal she had written for a 'pilot project' which was clearly an extension of the work I had initiated. Now that the respective Deputy Head had what Jane termed 'ownership', the achievement, Jane explained, would be 'sustainable' through a 'bubbling up' process.

More routinely, I took the initiative of telephoning some parents to remind them of parents' evenings, particularly those targeted for support. Data on attendance were not collated at either school; however, I was informed that the African Caribbean parents at the school tended to attend parents' evenings but that the phone calls 'seem to have done some good'. Parents seemed happy to receive the gentle prompt. On three occasions I was told that their child had not brought home the letter about the evening; and, on another, a parent who was unable to read expressed how pleased she was that I had called.

Beyond the school

Beyond the school, home visits formed another aspect of the role. I was asked to visit three boys who, prior to my arrival, had been excluded and sent to a Pupil Referral Unit, to 'find out what's happened to them'. On another occasion I initiated a home visit after consultation with the tutor due to the persistent truancy of a year 11 boy. Other parts of the role included 'troubleshooting', i.e. responding to 'emergency' situations from schools and parents, and training teachers. Almost too soon, the two terms were up and it was time to work as a Linkaid teacher at school two, Actmount.

School two: Actmount

At Actmount school, the intervention was mainly through being asked to focus on individual students, including keeping in regular contact with their families. During years 7 to 9 it was those 'causing concern', some of whom had already been temporarily excluded. For years 10 and above the support was more structured, in the form of being allocated specific students as part of the school's formal mentoring scheme. It was only relatively late in the proceedings that it was brought to my attention that the latter pupils were those the school had identified as being on the potential GCSE C/D borderline. Wambu and Brewster are the two families that will now be discussed in relation to the Linkaid role at Actmount school.

The Wambu family

'The mother is wonderful, a nurse, from Ghana. She works hard. The father died recently and left her with all boys', was the description of Mrs Wambu provided by the senior manager, Mrs Taylor, in our initial meeting where I was informed that Wambu would be one of the students I would be working with. The conversation highlighted that in being asked to support the child I was, in effect, being asked to support the mother.

All teachers used very positive and sympathetic language to describe Wambu's mother. When referring to Wambu, however, this type of language was absent. Conspicuous also by its absence was any mention of Wambu's academic ability or progress. Instead, Mrs Taylor informed me that 'he's a *very* good looking boy' (her emphasis). It was also mentioned, almost as an aside, that he 'had been stopped and searched by the police'.

Other unsolicited advice provided by Mrs Taylor was that 'the only way to deal with Wambu is quietly' together with the information that some teachers have described his attitude as 'dumb insolence'. Finally, I was informed that he had decided to change his name from Philip to Wambu and wanted to be called by that name. This was provided as a point of information, rather than with any suggestion of possible cultural connotations behind his decision.

Supporting the Wambu family

The first stage of my intervention, as negotiated, was that I would conduct classroom observations of lessons according to a schedule planned by Mrs Taylor. Discussions with the student, teacher and parent would follow.

Given the lack of focus on academic aspects it seemed significant that Wambu's opening remark during the first session was, 'I've got to catch up on what I've missed'. It was observed that he was very well equipped for his lesson, with others borrowing from the copious contents of his pencil case. He seemed intent on finishing his coursework although other students interrupted him at regular intervals with unrelated comments such as, 'Have you heard that song?' He completed well-written and carefully presented assignments, declaring 'I'm quite happy with that'.

'He can be quite sharp. He has an abrasive relationship with some, he's quite cocky ... a poor judge of when it's appropriate ... he shouts down the corridor.' These were the initial remarks when I explained to the teacher that I would be working with Wambu. Additionally, in a manner which appeared as a warning, when I reported that I had been asked by the Head of Year to be Wambu's mentor, the teacher related that Wambu was 'flirtatious' with female staff. These findings became more significant when, several months later, it was observed that Wambu was actively encouraged by the said member of staff to participate in a school concert playing the part of a young Adonis gyrating, with unbuttoned shirt, to Latin music, in a sexually explicit manner with one of the young female students in his year group. Whilst this was rationalised as 'just good fun' by staff and students alike, including Wambu, no other pupil had a similar role to play.

Moreover, in the considerable interaction with the student as a mentor, a 'flirtatious' manner was not observed. Indeed, I was treated with respect.

'Giving of her best'

When asked specifically about Wambu's academic ability the teacher reported a 'dual problem'. To elaborate: 'he gets confused and does find the work difficult but he doesn't do his bit. He's quite lazy and has admitted he's done little revision. He's often late.' The final remark by this teacher, who was also a senior manager, was not about Wambu but his mother. 'He has a bright mother, who's giving of her best.'

It turned out that her 'giving of her best' was under extremely difficult circumstances. These emerged piecemeal, during my involvement firstly as a Linkaid teacher and then when Mrs Wambu attended some of the Actionaid sessions. One difficulty was her professional schedule, which included working long hours, mainly night shifts. There were occasions when she contacted me on her arrival from the night shift prior to attempting to get some rest. On another occasion, she explained that she 'had an essay to do' and it transpired that she was undertaking professional studies in relation to her nursing job. Mrs Wambu asked that I keep her up to date with how Wambu was doing. Aside from the Actionaid meetings, the support, as with Mrs Clark, tended to consist of telephone conversations where I communicated the results of lesson observations etc. for Wambu; and later, for another son. Sometimes she telephoned me for advice. A salient example was her call saying she had only just learned that it was parents' evening for her younger son, who had special educational needs (another area in which she had asked for information and advice). He had not given her the form for her to select the teachers she wished to meet. I was able to liaise with the Head of Special Needs and, with the support of the Head of Year, managed to contact the teachers so that Mrs Wambu attended the sessions.

The support of the family extended to when Wambu received his examination results of four GCSEs at grade C and above (including one at B) and three at grade D. His mother related that he was upset because the Head of Sixth Form 'wouldn't let him into the sixth form, saying that his passes were weak passes so he had to resit at the local college … after that if he makes his mark he'll take him'. His mother said she was 'disappointed' explaining that she believed 'the school *could* take him because they know he can work hard, they saw how he was working near the end. I know he didn't actually sit down and do it properly from the beginning, he just got serious this term, and you helped him to do that'. Certainly, she and Wambu had been pleased when she had received a letter from the school commending Wambu on his improvement.

Wambu's initial response appeared more angry than upset, focusing on the fact that 'before, I was doing the foundation courses in French and

Science, then they jumped me up in the higher papers, I would *definitely* have got a C if I'd stayed with the foundation'. Having talked things through, his decision was to go to the college but not just to do retakes. His mother later reported that he was 'enjoying it at college'. A recent telephone call revealed that he had been successful in his college exams and is now back at Actmount school on advanced level courses.

The Brewster family

Home–school support centred on Brewster, a 16-year-old boy. The forthright comment from Mrs Taylor, the senior manager, indicating him as a student I would be working with, was that he's 'bone idle.' She added, 'he is also known to truant'.

This was perhaps the case where all three sides of the triangle – parent, child and teachers – had the most similarity of viewpoint. 'He sits by my side in the front as it's the only way I can get any work out of him. Needs a shove to get him going' was an equally candid comment, written by a different teacher on a 'progress check' for my attention as his mentor. Under the section for homework was: 'You must be joking, it's like getting blood out of a stone.' Later, it emerged that Brewster had entered the school after what his mother described as 'being excluded from another school for smoking weed last year'. She expressed the view that 'he's never done it since'.

In supporting Brewster, the Head of Year allocated me as his mentor as part of their general school programme to support all students on the C/D borderline. This included regular sessions with students to listen to any concerns and negotiate targets according to their needs. After the initial session, where we discussed the reasons behind Brewster leaving his last school, examination of the mentor targets included items such as 'planning and organising workloads so as to prevent falling behind – needs to catch up on geography and maths'. On another occasion, after the school discovered his truancy, this formed the focus of the mentoring session.

'It's a struggle for me'

The Linkaid and mentoring role included keeping in regular contact with the family, with reports of progress, praise or concerns. Mrs Brewster described her son as 'very laid back ... I don't know why he's like that. It's a mixture of stuff. It's for everything. He can spend how many minutes ironing a shirt'. She added, 'he smiles sweetly at me and thinks he can get away with things'. Like the teachers, she was concerned that he would not obtain the grades he was capable of. She related how she had taken the week off work when Brewster was on study leave. In an effort to get him to work she had, she said, cooked him all his favourite meals. He woke up in time to eat but 'did not do any work'.

'It's a struggle for me because I feel on my own and I have to be the educator, the person who finds everything out, the person who sorts things out.' She described her children as 'mixed race'. Their father was a Black American man 'who's not here, he's chosen not to take any interest in his son but I've told Brewster to try to find out about the rest of his family if he wants to'. Her own father she said was 'an academic, he's got a very good reputation in his field'.

In the school-based mentoring role Brewster told me how he 'liked going up to London' to see his sister and 'hang out with her boyfriend ... He's Black and really into music and all that'. It also become apparent from discussion with Brewster and his mother that Brewster and his friends regularly spent a great deal of their time at Brewster's home 'mixing' music.

On discussing her son's truancy, Mrs Brewster stated: 'he's happier when he's not at school. His shoulders rise up when he has to go ... He *does* want to go college, whatever he does best in.' One of the strategies used in the Linkaid role was to negotiate with Brewster, in conjunction with the Head of Year, that he could 'drop' a subject that he had already indicated that he 'can't stand' if he were to attend school on a regular basis and on time and would use the time to complete coursework for his other subjects. Subsequent meetings and telephone contact with his mother suggested that this helped him to become more motivated at school. Brewster's GCSE results were mainly grade D and E which he described as 'alright' and he is now at college.

Key emergent themes

The following sections highlight some significant issues gleaned from the home–school liaison, action research.

The four students, like most of those I was asked to support, were boys. An extract of a letter from a head teacher outlines the nature of the 'problem' from his perspective:

> In the case of some boys, they could ideally do with a male teacher to look at their attitudes to white authority.
>
> (Letter to Multicultural Education Centre from the school)

Since the head teacher had left by the time I arrived, it was not possible to probe him directly. Instead, I attempted to unravel the different levels of meaning. I considered the possible meaning if the phrase were simply: 'They could ideally do with a male teacher' or 'to look at their attitudes to authority.' Its explicit statement of the boys' needs 'to look at their attitude to *white* authority' appears to reflect a particular stance to race relations and expectations that Linkaid would not only concur with but promote his stance.

Once at the school, no other instances of such *explicit* language of expectations were cited. However, at both schools, the proportion of African and Caribbean boys observed outside of the classrooms, having been sent out by the teacher, or outside the office of a member of the senior leadership team, was more than that of any other group. For target pupils and, where time permitted, for others, I would ask the reason for them being outside the classroom. Invariably, the reason could have been encapsulated under the phrase 'attitude toward white authority'. For those students being supported, if it proved to be more than a single incident, or a regular occurrence with a specific teacher, this was followed up where possible.

The following response from a middle manager reveals her response upon being asked to provide information about the children in her year group:

> *Paul*
> Chip on shoulder about things. A very bright lad, very able. Feels he's been picked on by some of the staff. Mum a very powerful lady; hot on rights, feels it's racist.
> (African Caribbean, year 9)

> *Tony*
> A leader, unusual character, sly, bright enough to do it in an underhand way and to get away with it. A very powerful boy. A very big body, good at sport.
> (Dual heritage, year 9)

> *Errol*
> One of the lads, very popular with boys and girls
> (African Caribbean, year 9)

It became apparent that even when assessment data indicated that the boys were perceived as being of high or above average ability, this was not mentioned to me. Instead, this aspect was usually submerged within other more negative characteristics, as with Paul, above. Another feature was some teachers, usually but not always women, on being asked to provide information about the boys, tended to use adjectives and phrases to depict their physical appearance. Tony being described as 'A very powerful boy, a very big body' was echoed in similar 'information' at both schools. 'Statuesque', '*very* good looking' [the teacher's emphasis] was another example, from Actdale School. The case of Wambu was the most overt sexual reference, for example the use of the word 'flirtatious'. Across the cases, however, even very young boys, from year 8 upward, were being depicted by staff as implicitly sexualised. An academically able, mixed heritage boy who had been described by his Head of Year as 'beautiful' was, for example, permanently excluded for 'inappropriate sexual misconduct' with reference to another pupil. His mother, whom I was asked to contact to offer support *after* the decision to exclude, pointed out that 'the other two boys, both white, were not excluded'. At both schools, all but one case of exclusions was a boy.

The words and actions demonstrated by some of the teachers toward the boys conveyed quite a range of complex features that proved difficult to categorise as one particular stance. At Actmount school, the senior manager responsible for students in years 7 to 9 repeatedly referred to 'my boys'. Another stance, almost of gentle acknowledgement of a propensity toward being 'bone idle', was seen with Brewster and others. This contrasted with the teacher whose students consistently obtained higher grades, with Wambu obtaining a B and Brewster, one of his highest grades. It was noted that even when Wambu showed signs of improvement, she praised him but continued to discuss other aspects of his work that would need to be developed if he were to receive the grade he wanted.

'Doesn't realise how powerful she is'

In one of the above examples, it was noted that 'Paul's mum' was described as a 'very powerful lady'. Whenever the word 'powerful', was used, it was not in a context considered by male or female teachers to be a positive characteristic of either a child or parent. Teachers describing girls and mothers who were perceived as problems used this adjective repeatedly. A female Head of Year in another case, for example, described one of the girls as 'quite powerful for her group of friends' and explained that she 'can influence a group of people. Doesn't realise how *powerful* she is' (her emphasis). This was immediately followed by, 'Got a really *nice* side', the implication being that being 'powerful' is somehow not 'nice'. Similarly, note the thumbnail sketch the Linkaid teacher/researcher was given of Davinia:

> She's difficult. Mum's a very powerful lady and will support her. I've never actually met her but she's well known to [another Head of Year] and to people who've been here longer than me. She's [Davinia] aggressive with other kids in the playground and has been in fights. In class she's more sensible, she tells off kids who aren't listening.

It was useful to consider the adjectives employed to describe Davinia: 'powerful', 'aggressive', 'She likes to fight'. Her mother was also described as a 'powerful lady'. The sexuality of the girls was not usually referred to in the way that the boys was, but often their size was, and frequently in conjunction with their 'power'. Like the boys, the school concentrated on all factors apart from the academic. A telling example was the teacher emphasising Davinia's actions out of class. An alternative approach could have built on Davinia's wish to become more involved in her studies, whilst still using appropriate sanctions when she was involved in fights. When it was suggested that I could 'work with' Davinia or 'contact her mum' it was on no occasion in relation to her studies; instead it was over her 'aggressive behaviour'. The account by the teacher portrays another common theme, for both parents and pupils. The teacher, relatively new to the school, had not yet met Davinia's mother but was already negatively disposed toward her, due to information from other teachers.

It became quite striking just how rare it was for girls to be included in the list for Linkaid support. When this was raised with an Actmount senior manager, the line manager of Linkaid, by pointing out, on first being given the list: 'oh, I notice they're all boys', the response was agreement and that the students were those found to be 'causing concern'. She added, 'this is in line with national trends'.

Over a period of time, having worked closely with the allocated students, I approached Heads of Year indicating that I was considering extending the number of students and asked for suggestions as to students whom they would consider able to benefit from such support. It was at this stage, not on the initiative of the school, that girls such as Davinia were mentioned. Neither was there a female equivalent of Brewster's type of support, i.e. someone provided with support due to being considered by the staff to be 'bone idle'. At school two there was, instead, one example of an African Caribbean female student, Folashi, who was cited as being 'one of our best' and that 'ideally she could do with some cultural input, she's the only Black girl in the class'. It was suggested, however, that in order to prioritise my time, she should not be in the 'official' list for my support as part of the mentoring scheme but it would be helpful if I could provide a mentor through my involvement with Actionaid.

'I should be able to get a C'

Wambu, Clark, and others not in the case studies and some of their parents, referred on several occasions to working 'to get a C'. They had gathered from the school that this was an important aim. Chamberlain and his mother in common with girls like Folashi, whom I met via my home–school role, did not however speak in terms of C grade as an ultimate target but wanted to 'get the highest grade I can'. Like Wambu, some of the boys aiming for a C grade obtained Ds. Wambu especially was disappointed, saying for one subject, 'I really thought I'd get a C in that'. Chamberlain received some B grades. Brewster explained, 'I knew I didn't work hard enough to get my Cs'. As a school, the girls, who had received much less support, obtained much better results.

'I'm white, my husband is Black'

Unexpectedly, a relatively higher proportion of the list of students had parents of dual ethnic ancestry. Both Mrs Chamberlain and Mrs Brewster referred to issues relating to parenting their children as white mothers. Mrs Chamberlain was a particularly interesting parent in unravelling the implications of this, given her own description of her family background:

> I'm white, my husband is Black. My two previous children are white. With Chamberlain, I try to understand his culture because I think I need to know about it. But it's almost like teachers in school, they don't understand. When you come to school it's a white culture.

It was Mrs Chamberlain who made the recommendation at the achievement evening that the school should have assemblies with a focus on Black role models and include Black history and culture as part of 'normal lessons'. She was also quite categorical in her insistence that what she termed police harassment of her son when he was out in the local area was racially motivated and stated that 'this never happened' to her white son when he was living in the same area. Although both Mrs Chamberlain and Mrs Brewster were white British mothers with children whose fathers were Black American, Mrs Chamberlain referred to her son as Black whilst Mrs Brewster called her son 'mixed race' and as their case studies reveal, their parenting styles and home–school relations were very different.

A local head teacher, on learning about my work with parents, suggested informally that for pupils of mixed heritage, this was:

> more of an issue for Black children with white mums where more often the mums haven't really taken cultural issues in hand. Where they attempt to show their child some side of their culture ... what they can't do is anything about their experiences.

She added that most of the difficulties were 'to do with other people' and that 'teachers and the mum don't always understand'. She suggested that we provide specific training on this issue. In another instance a local school was contacted over a complaint to the Multicultural Educational Service (MES) from an African Caribbean parent that her daughter and other Black children at the school were being 'picked on and labelled as a group'. My role in this instance was intended to be more of a mediating stance. The initial response of the Head of Year was to say 'I've got two biracial children myself and I feel that's not the case'.

It transpired that Miranda was also the parent of 'two biracial children'. As part of a discussion on racism, and one of the few occasions when she described herself as 'Black', she said, 'I can quote myself as an example'.

> I was the only Black person living in the village and was ignored by the other parents outside the school gates ... . When my children were

called racist names I asked to take assembly or do supply teaching but these offers were declined.

From a child's perspective, it was Chamberlain who made some particularly noteworthy comments:

> When you are a Black ... African, Caribbean ... child it's more the norm for you stick out, Black people are just used to sticking out
>
> [Researcher: How do you think the school sees you in terms of ethnicity?]
>
> I think they just see me as Black. I'm too much trouble to be white.

At Actdale school, the teachers referred to Chamberlain as Black, unlike some of the other 'mixed-heritage' children. Like the few other Black children in the school, Chamberlain did 'stick out' in that during the weekly classroom observations, covering different students being supported, it was almost exclusively the case that Black students were either the only Black child in the class or with only one or at the most two others. Chamberlain did not wish to pursue his statement of why he should be 'too much trouble to be white' but when contextualised with his other views it suggested that was his perception of what the *teachers* thought. Moreover, this accorded with the requests for my support over the 'trouble' being caused in terms of his behaviour.

'What language do they speak in Jamaica?'

The above question was asked of me by a teacher at Actdale school, the same school where a Head of Year described a boy as having 'the thickest Jamaican accent I've ever heard'. Issues of language and dialect formed part of my troubleshooting role at other schools. In all such instances where I was asked to support, pupils had recently arrived from Jamaica. They had been living in rural communities and the schools did not have records of their schooling. Some of the staff, when unable to comprehend the dialect, were unsure whether the children's needs were cognitive or linguistic. Another such occasion necessitated responding to a teacher who had written to the MES requesting support over assessing the language needs of some newly arrived Jamaican boys, as well as books 'relevant to their culture'. Part of the school's request was that I should conduct classroom observations followed by informal conversations with the pupils. It was not difficult to establish that, cognitively, they were fine. I did, however, suggest some specific generic features of teaching and learning including subject-specific vocabulary as well as basic classroom management issues such as the most appropriate room layout and position to aid the boys' learning. I also provided information on suitable texts. The support to schools in such situations was an attempt to respond to their needs and to counteract basic misconceptions about language and society in the Caribbean as it related to the young persons and their family. Initial support of the parents included providing a context in which the boys and their family could share experiences and express needs and felt comfortable using dialect amidst their use of Standard English.

During the Linkaid role, special educational needs emerged as an issue more often than anticipated. Linguistic issues, as above, were found to be associated with the children being placed on the SEN register, with another dominant reason being behaviour. An accompanying finding was that the parents did not seem to be fully conversant with the SEN regulations and how this applied to their child.

The nature of the role of an EMAG funded teacher is worth pointing to here. The school-based Linkaid teacher referred to it thus:

'I'm doing this job with Black status'

I've always done this job with white status but here I'm doing this job with Black status and I can see the difference and it's incredible the differences you *have* in terms of the way that you're perceived.

Her explanation centred on being afforded some professional respect when she undertook similar jobs in places like India, and that in comparison, such 'non-mainstream' posts in the UK are accorded a relatively low status.

In common with most of the encounters with LEA services, employees in senior management were white. The 'Black and bilingual' employees, on the evidence of information at team meetings, training sessions and interaction with a range of staff, were positioned such that they could provide a resource for the other employees learning from them about Black and bilingual issues. The expectations on these staff in relation to their input about Black and bilingual issues seemed, at the very least, unrealistic. At school one, in the handbook describing our work with Black and bilingual families, I was the *only* team member who was described in terms of having 'responsibility' for a group of pupils, i.e. African and Caribbean pupils, despite the part-time nature of my appointment.

Analysis of the work of colleagues suggested that there was less scope for the 'Black and bilingual' staff to become involved in more mainstream activities. If the 'Black and bilingual' staff were encouraged to attend or deliver training, it was less likely to be of a more mainstream nature. One of the consequences of this seemed to be that, having learned from their Black and bilingual colleagues, some white members of the MES seemed to position themselves as 'experts' on Black and bilingual issues as well as the wider educational issues. The Black staff, not having as much opportunity for mainstream professional development, appeared more marginalised. It is interesting to note in this respect the words of the area manager (who was at middle management level) about her own experience: 'I was not given a teaching job in Actford when I first moved down here because I was Black'. The history of the African Caribbean post holders suggests that not only are they less likely to be *in situ* when appointed, they are more likely to leave than the other ethnic groups. This was the case with my predecessor, whom, I was informed, was the first African Caribbean male to be appointed. As Jane, the Linkaid representative at the school, states: 'his contribution was minimised'. Although, according to her, this may be an inevitable consequence of the nature of the post where as Linkaid/EMAG funded teachers we are in effect raising awareness and 'giving ownership' to other teachers to sustain. The cumulative effect of 'giving ownership' marginalisation and lack of access to more mainstream professional development opportunities was a predominantly white British workforce, except at the least senior positions.

Linkaid: facilitating and constraining factors

'You sound just like my sister'

Being a Black woman with understanding of issues as they relate to the Black community was viewed as an asset by most of the parents I was working with. This was indicated in quite basic ways such as when first telephoning a parent with whom I had previously had face-to-face contact, being given a warm reception on the basis that 'you sound just like my sister'.

In several conversations, reference was made to many types of issues experienced by Black families, not always directly connected with school matters, for instance their young male children being stopped regularly by the police, and on occasions I was asked not to reveal this information to the school. Other personal information included financial aspects including those that had implications for supporting their child's education. Brewster had two part-time jobs, Wambu worked some evenings and just prior to his GCSEs became involved, through Brewster's mother, with a course for which he was paid to attend. When informed about a child whose job on a number of days per week meant that he 'gets home around 10', I was cautious about making any suggestions that he could perhaps work fewer evenings given the imminence of forthcoming exams. An unexpected finding was that in spite of their circumstances, many of the parents, both men and women, were 'studying too' as one parent stated. This ranged from counselling, to degrees, aromatherapy and furniture restoration. At school, staff did not generally have this type of background knowledge.

'You have to remember that you are working for the school'

> There is always conflict because of the dual role of HSL [home–school liaison] and teacher. You have to remember that you are working for the school.

Miranda, the area team manager, provided the above words of advice. Manoeuvring the 'dual role' proved an enormous constraint at times. This was especially difficult when attempting to provide the support the parents sought in matters of conflict between themselves and the school. Even more difficult were cases of complaints against specific teachers, particularly as during the course of work certain teachers' names arose from a number of different parents as a cause for concern. Some of those teachers had positions of responsibility and influence. At Actdale, relations that a number of African and Caribbean families had with two Heads of Year seemed to be characterised by conflict and a mutual lack of respect. The majority of the parents and children referred to one name and to a lesser extent another Head of Year in very negative terms and several gave examples of behaviour they described as racist. Some contrasted these attitudes with other Heads of Year and staff with whom they had more constructive relations.

As a Linkaid teacher I needed to be quite strategic about augmenting those issues which, from the perspective of the school, needed to be addressed, with the requirements of the parents and the child. This was helped by insider professional knowledge and experience resulting in a confidence, recognised by a senior manager who expressed the view that 'you clearly know what you're doing'. The result was that I was afforded flexibility within the role and was able to negotiate strategic targets. A pertinent example is the achievement evening organised at Actdale. I had been informed from the onset that although the African Caribbean parents tended to attend parents' evenings, they were not, in general, greatly involved in the life of the school. Where the incorporation of targets for Linkaid could be combined within the priorities of the School Development Plan and the MES this provided a more explicit connection. Equally, I was able to embed the support within the existing structures and priorities for GCSE mentoring at Actmount, working closely with the Head of Year organising the scheme.

The role of the SLT and Heads of Year: 'A good thing'

As a survival strategy, especially at Actdale, it was vital to gain the support of the head teacher and senior leadership team in general. More unexpectedly, support from the Heads of Year was found to facilitate my role in meeting the needs of the families. They were in an influential position as they received, from subject teachers and form tutors, information concerning academic, behavioural and general pastoral issues, including family-related matters. For those families with children in year 11, their role was especially important. The Heads of Year could be both a force for constructive support, 'pushing', cajoling or urging students toward greater and more effective academic effort, or a force for alienating the students, and parents, still further. Several students echoed Chamberlain's view that 'whenever they hear anything, it's always something bad'. As Chamberlain's case highlights, their role was also extensive in relation to access to post-16 studies, via references to these institutions. An increased understanding of the importance of the Head of Year was heightened because of the sharp contrast which existed between the schools in this respect. The Head of Year I liaised with at Actmount school appeared to have in-depth knowledge of and *care* about the students and their parents as individuals *and* was able to appreciate their academic, social and cultural needs. In discussing some Linkaid activities she states:

> Certainly with the boys who've been involved in that group, people like Chamberlain and Brewster have thought about it very positively and I think that anything that helps to raise their profile within the school and their sense of pride in their culture and their achievement is a good thing.

Analysis of her role in different cases leaves it unclear whether it is the teacher's personal qualities of demonstrating respect, openness and a constructive attitude toward others and to cultural diversity or if it is her interpretation of the way to conduct the professional role of Head of Year. The outcome, however, was that her interaction with students and parents that others found 'difficult' tended to be relatively smooth. No parent had a negative word to say about their interaction with her and certainly her attitude helped to facilitate my Linkaid role at the school.

'You have been there for me, you were helping me because there was a need'

The tensions involved in negotiating the duality of the role were never completely diminished. As the above discussions reveal, I attempted, where feasible, to circumvent many of the barriers. I prioritised the limited time on situations where I felt I could make a difference, maximising the facilitating forces, including concentrating on working in a constructive manner with teachers with the characteristics of Iris, and Jane, the Head of Year; and providing parents with information about school and exam processes. Some parents were quite astute at recognising the position I was in and the extent of the circumstances where I was able to help. As one commented, 'To make sure that you're still given information about what you need to know for the pupils and us, the parents, you need to keep low.' I will leave the last word to the said parent, not one of the case studies due to her wish for confidentiality, whom I assisted over issues regarding her son and one of the schools:

> I was looking around and thinking who's here for me here. Before there was no one. Thank you Lorna, you have been there for me, you were helping me because there was a need.

Implications for schools

'More focused on schooling than ... on discipline' has to be the starting point for the lessons we learn about promoting pupil achievement and, indeed, for involving the parents. If we interpret this as focusing on challenging pupils intellectually, as Mrs Chamberlain told the school from 'day one', we note that even Brewster managed to obtain his highest grade from a teacher who did just that, the one who 'pushed' Wambu in his pursuit of the grade he was capable of. The pupils had imbibed the school's mantra of the need to obtain a C grade but some interpreted this as a 'ceiling of C', which left them unchallenged intellectually.

Manifestations of behaviour that the school construed as an 'attitude to white authority' by either the pupil or parents, was unlikely to be left unchallenged. The letter stating categorically that 'some of the boys, they could ideally do with a male teacher to look at their attitudes to white authority' suggests almost an *expectation* of conflict, which becomes a self-fulfilling prophecy. This instance shows the effects of a school culture where teachers feel confident enough to consistently describe boys in primarily stereotypical terms of having a 'chip on his shoulder' with overt displays of racism, knowing that they would be left unchallenged. Girls and mothers with powerful characteristics, and those who 'feel' that their treatment is racist would also be construed as having 'an attitude to white authority'. A focus more on schooling (interpreted by me as learning) than on discipline is likely to have improved the situation at this school, with its high rate of exclusions and poor examination results. A different approach may have been able to draw on the 'power' of the pupils and parents to a more positive effect.

It is just such an approach that Iris, another Linkaid colleague, demonstrated. Rather than the above expectation of a certain attitude toward 'white authority', Iris went out of her way to understand and learn about the culture of the students she was working with. This included finding culturally relevant websites and other material to motivate them to achieve their very best. In a classroom setting, observing Iris in operation is instructive. She urged pupils quietly toward greater efforts, having carefully analysed assessment data. She knew them as individuals, not just in terms of their work, and had an understanding of their family background. This type of knowledge and understanding would clearly preclude thinking about and speaking of pupils and their families in the stereotypical or racist terms we saw earlier. As a 'reflective practitioner' Iris also kept up to date with research in many areas, including cultural and linguistic issues, and used this to enhance her own learning and better meet the pupils' needs. The question 'what language do they speak in Jamaica?' is unlikely to have been asked of a teacher with the personal and professional qualities of Iris.

At another level of seniority, the Head of Year at Actmount school is an exemplar of the professional qualities required of a Head of Year interacting with pupils and parents in today's diverse society and highlights the importance of the role of Head of Year which could either help or hamper both achievement and effective home–school relations.

Making pupils 'responsible for their own learning' appears to work for pupils like Chamberlain and others, gifted but whom the parents and teachers acknowledge 'can be a handful'. I was able to observe the difference in learning and behaviour of the same pupils in classes with teachers where they were so absorbed in their work that behaviour was never an issue.

This day-to-day presence in different classrooms highlighted most profoundly the need for schools to be able to share the good practice within their school, in fact within the same departments sometimes, on ways in which they could promote the good behaviour of their pupils and the type of classroom environment and pedagogical practice that foster effective learning. This was especially the case with pupils whom we know, as Mrs Chamberlain recognises, can be 'a handful', 'rude' and 'offensive'. Like Mrs Chamberlain, we can 'understand how a teacher can be frustrated'. I am not recommending here that schools should ignore such behaviour. We also recognise the need for school rules, such as being 'back from lunch at a certain time'. The potential effects of teaching a pupil with an 'attitude' of 'I'm not going to respect them just because they're teachers' cannot be ignored.

What daily observations of the different lessons allows one to understand most dramatically, however, and would allow teachers with consistent difficulties in this area to see in practice, is that some teachers have a range of strategies and the type of personal and professional qualities that defuse any potential for challenging behaviour which in another class escalates. Even the 'amiable' Clark, had 'trouble' with a particular teacher to the extent that it impacted on his learning as he did not wish to move up a set in maths which would require being taught by the said teacher.

A flexible approach to the curriculum was beneficial in supporting some pupils. In the case of Brewster, for example, with only a few months before exams, we negotiated that he could 'drop' some subjects and use the time to complete coursework in subjects where he would be most likely to achieve success. This provided an incentive for him to work. In providing this extra 'push' I was also supporting teachers and his mother, who were 'finding it a struggle' to keep him motivated. The image of his 'shoulders rising up' at the prospect of going to school is telling. More time in the Linkaid role or support from other agencies may have led to a better appreciation of why, and more opportunity to find solutions.

Schools and parents clearly need a better understanding of each other. This was as basic as 'what language do they speak in Jamaica?' to the ways in which life may be 'a struggle' for these families. Understanding the conflicting demands on the parents: evening-shifts, studying, financial constraints, for example, is more likely to lead to teachers who do not equate non-attendance at parents' evening as 'uninvolved' and may provide a more flexible approach to timing of meetings including meeting individually where necessary. Keeping things 'under the carpet' at parents' evenings and other times was unhelpful to all.

More informal activities, like the achievement session, helped to develop more constructive relationships and to build trust. For trust in the school and its systems to develop, parents need to feel confident that if they 'went through the right channels' as Clark and even Chamberlain and his family tried, the head teacher would act appropriately, including challenging the behaviour of teachers, like the one who was the catalyst for Chamberlain's last straw, whose negative characteristics were acknowledged by even ex-pupils, and where racism compounded its effects. Parents were prepared to challenge their children's behaviour and 'stick up for' the school and believed that the school should do likewise, for example challenging teachers and 'sticking up' for the pupil where necessary, as had occurred in one instance.

The need for attention to the specific needs of parents of 'mixed heritage' children was an unexpected issue emerging from the case and is an area that some parents and teachers have suggested that the schools and the Local Authority have given insufficient attention. It was evident that parents with children of mixed heritage, and their children, appreciated my support. This is perhaps exemplified most powerfully in the interaction with Mrs Chamberlain and her family. She reported that 'Chamberlain was right upset that Marvin got you [as a mentor] and he was given Mrs X'. Mrs X was a white British teacher whom I knew was respected by Chamberlain.

Notwithstanding the above, it is suggested that schools may need to develop their understanding of the needs of families where pupils are of mixed heritage as their distinct needs may be obscured under the more general interventions in promoting home–school liaison as one of the strategies for raising the attainment of pupils at risk of underachieving.

Similarly, school practice that, quite rightly, tries to focus on intervening in high exclusions or underachievement of Black boys may inadvertently neglect the underachievement of Black girls.

The language used by the teachers is an area worthy of attention in considering classroom practice. Some of the teachers who provided information about the pupils were clearly unaware of how negative the general portrayal of the Black pupils sounded or that their language could be perceived as racist. The 'inadvertent' language of cultural stereotyping was perhaps more evident in the way some teachers described Black boys. Any judgment or sanctions including exclusions against the conduct of Black boys would need to avoid racial stereotyping in the context of their masculinity.

The 'generalised' nature of the language used to refer to reasons for exclusions is an area with potential implications for schools. A critical case involves a child being excluded for 'sexually inappropriate misconduct'. I was not provided with the full details. Anybody however, whether a parent, colleague or member of a governing body, seeing this on a document or hearing about it would be aware that 'sexually inappropriate misconduct' is a disturbing, emotionally charged issue and one that a school would need to take very seriously indeed. A 'lesson learned' from this case is that school leaders, perhaps with the help of support agencies, may need to consider ways of providing clarity in specific cases and have a shared approach to what constitutes 'sexually inappropriate misconduct', ideally framed within wider codes of conduct and policies highlighting what is or is not appropriate for pupils *and* staff.

Implications for home–school liaison support

The major learning in this chapter is that the tensions in attempting to meet the needs of the pupil, family and school are immense but so are the opportunities for support. With a pragmatic, strategic and flexible approach, it was possible to use inside professional knowledge as a teacher to support the pupils' learning and provide wider information and advice to parents and families about school and cultural issues over which they sought support. My cultural knowledge and understanding as a Black woman of African Caribbean ancestry was a factor at least as important as my professional knowledge in meeting the needs of the families.

Matters of conflict between parents and schools were difficult aspects of the role with parents' allegations of the racism of specific teachers the most challenging area. The main challenge was that the interpretation of 'partnership' between the Multicultural Education Service and the schools in which the home–school liaison staff were based, was that in reality, 'you're working for the school'. It would seem necessary at LEA level to develop appropriately independent 'channels' for action in such situations.

This would clearly seem to be the case in matters of school exclusions. If the home–school liaison worker is 'working for the school' and particularly if the role itself is seen by the school as having 'Black status' and is therefore marginalised, the potential for providing the type of support that the families may consider necessary is limited.

Where the home–school liaison support does have more of an influence is in providing the kind of actions that may help to prevent situations from escalating to the point of exclusions. The type of interventions used in this role had some similarity to that provided by Learning Mentors on a day-to-day basis for areas in receipt of such designated funding. It offers scope for further support to schools by using their experience to deliver on-site training in matters such as promoting positive behaviour, especially of the more 'challenging' pupils, and working constructively with a range of parents to understand and meet their requirements and help their children to focus on learning. The work at Actdale in beginning to develop a shared understanding of the respective role of the parent, child and school is an area worthy of further exploration by schools.

It was possible in some circumstances for the home–school liaison role to work for the benefit of all three parties toward the mutual goal of raising achievement. The success of the parents' achievement session showed that Actdale school was able to learn about 'what works' in organising events that encourage Black parents to attend, and where many of the benefits have been sustainable. For some aspects, however, it was found necessary to develop a parent support group independent of schools, as described in the following chapter.

Chapter 4

Actionaid: 'We need to know'

A community-based Black parents' group

Actionaid: Community-based action research project

Actionaid is a voluntary, community-based parent support organisation set up by the researcher, with a collection of parents. The parents were met, in the first instance through schools and the local community during my employment as a home–school liaison teacher. It aims to support parents of African and Caribbean children in supporting their children's education and ally their needs with that of the school, and the action research opportunities afforded by the role.

The context and rationale of the project

Following the success of the achievement session at Actdale, the first school, several of the parents expressed the view that they wished the session to progress to a group where parents could meet on a regular basis but they did not wish the sessions to be school based. Instead, they wanted a forum for the parents to meet that was independent of the school, one in which Black children who were attending any school in the locality would be able to participate. The views of the local African Caribbean families were sought by the researcher at the stage of identification of issues from their perspective. Having clarified the questions, issues and goals of parents, I was in a position to link these to the aims and requirements of the research project. Decisions were then made concerning the most appropriate types of interventions or specific actions to be taken. The main and most important action was clearly to set up the parent support group.

The process of setting up the group

Although the process of setting up the group is worthy of a study in itself, a summary of the key features follows.

While some of the parents had previous knowledge of how community organisations work, based on volunteer activities and membership of another management committee, neither I nor any of the other members had ever been involved in establishing a formal community organisation from scratch. It was decided that we could still proceed in our actions, meeting informally while finding out how to formalise the working of the group. This proved to be an appropriate course of action since it responded to the parents' wish to set things in motion quite quickly. 'What are we waiting for, as long as we have somewhere to meet' was one of the comments. The 'somewhere to meet' was the local community centre, a Council owned and managed facility which turned out, on enquiry, to be free to local voluntary groups. This fact was especially important at this stage, as the group had no financial resources.

Having obtained a range of material from textual and computer-based sources on how to set up, run and manage voluntary organisations, one of the first ports of call on a formal basis, to supplement informal discussions with known voluntary groups, was the local branch of a national organisation aimed at providing advice to voluntary organisations. An appointment was made with one of the key members during a period of her 'advice surgeries'. Advice included 'start small' and 'be clear about your aims', most of which the group had already discussed. I was aware, however, that some key information was provided only after I had asked the appropriate question, on the basis of information already gleaned from books and earlier informal research. An important example was asking about the different types of constitution. Although the person conducting the advice surgery provided a summary of this, it was only when I asked whether she had a copy of a model constitution that this was supplied. This model was used as a basis for customising our own aims and objectives into its formal requirements. This was an ongoing procedure, with revisions made with input from the groups at our monthly meetings. Having a constitution later proved to be an important requirement for funding bodies awarding grants. Given that we were unpaid volunteers and the accommodation for meetings was free, the group was able to start off self-financed and over a period of time obtained small grants to cover costs such as telephone, stationery, refreshments and guest speakers.

How the organisation was established

From its initial informal discussions of issues raised by the group, in line with the requirements of the constitution, the structure changed to be set up as a management committee. The minimum requirement was the election of a chairperson, secretary and treasurer with other members being co-opted for various roles. It proved to be difficult to persuade parents to put themselves forward for election to the Chair. Some said things to the effect that they 'don't mind helping out, but would prefer it to be behind the scenes'. It was only much later that one of them admitted that 'we thought you should have been the Chair'. I had stated at the onset that 'it would be good if one of the parents were Chair' giving reasons such as 'I don't want the group to be seen as *my* group'. Essentially, I believed that it was more empowering to the group if a parent had the position of Chairperson. Second, the position of Chair would not have afforded me the same opportunity for observation, reflection and review as the less 'hands on' position of secretary. In the event, two local parents became Chair and treasurer respectively with me as secretary. Although structured in this manner, in effect, the actions and processes to be used in supporting the parents were decided on a group basis, according to the expressed needs of the parents.

The families within the twelve core members cover a cross-section of social class, educational background and family construction. They include, at two extremes, a parent undertaking a postgraduate professional degree and one who is unable to read. The parents' ages range from early twenties to late thirties, plus two grandparents, who are older. Their children were mainly at secondary schools (aged 11–18) in the local area, with the exception of one 10-year-old child in a primary school. Although these families form the core, other families were also involved on a more intermittent basis for other activities.

Key issues arising from the parents

'You need to know'

Mrs Clark, one of the original members of the group, explained,

> You need to know what's going on within the school. I think parents need to know because they're there just for parents' evening, you don't see what's under the carpet, everything's on the surface and you get smiles. Everybody's chatting to you and you don't know what's underlying that and *especially* Black parents [her emphasis] they *do* need to know.

The phrase, 'you need to know' encapsulates the concerns of those attending Actionaid. One of the first stages in responding to the parents' needs was to glean, from the data emerging from individual and group discussions, the incidents where it was stated directly that they 'need to know' and the types of matters they said they 'need to know' about. Before discussing these, the phrase 'especially Black parents' is considered.

'Especially Black parents'

The '*especially* Black parents' phrase turned out to be one that deepened in its noteworthiness. The original concept of the group was that it was for Black parents; or more precisely, African and Caribbean parents, starting with those who had originally expressed the need for such a group. While the majority of the core group of parents attending the monthly sessions were Black – in effect, African and Caribbean – white parents with British children where the other parent was Black, usually African Caribbean or African American, were involved from the very beginning, since, as one of the African Caribbean parents stated, 'their children are going to face some of the things *we* have to deal with'. The significance of the phrase at one level was that the organisation was one that was set up '*especially* for Black parents' but did not exclude other groups. A full consideration of why the parents deemed it necessary 'especially for Black parents' will be better appreciated after the discussion of the types of matter the parents considered they needed to know about and how the organisation attempted to meet their needs.

Supporting the need to know: education and school processes

Initially, specific mention of need was directly related to school aspects. The dominant need covered items directly related to the courses and examinations their children were undertaking. These included, to use the parents' phrase, both 'surface' and 'underlying' matters. Although, on prompting, the parents said that some schools had provided written brochures outlining, for example, SATs and GCSE criteria, most reported that it was often too late by the time that the parents realised the implications for their own children's examinations. As the parents had children of different age groups, those with younger children were able to learn from the types of issues being raised by others. A common request, as at Linkaid, was how and where to obtain past examination papers.

> I've been asking the school for past exam papers for months and it is like a problem getting them. Every time he goes to a lesson I say have you asked the teachers about the papers. They tell him I'll give it to you next time, I haven't got one at the moment ... what do you want it for, who's going to mark the papers. That's my problem Lorna, if I'm asking for the papers. It's good to get an idea of what to expect for an exam. It doesn't matter whether the child is actually getting the work marked, it just gives them a general rough idea of what's going to take place. It's like talking to school kids to be honest with you, in one ear and out the other.

The above parent, like all the parents in the study, was very keen to support her child's education. Even if she knew that she lacked the specific knowledge of a subject she was aware of the need to have an understanding of the exam requirements to monitor her child's work. This parent and others were supported by the delivery of a workshop training session specifically related to these types of issues. In planning for the workshop, however, I explained to the parent that the exam syllabi were organised by a few exam boards and that it would be necessary to get up-to-date information. We shared the telephoning that was necessary and eventually we obtained the information and made it available to the rest of the group.

More so than at Linkaid, underlying matters, those described as being swept 'under the carpet', were also raised by the participants. One parent, for example, asked: 'How do they decide which exams to put the children in?' It transpired in a meeting that the parents in the study were aware that the school expected them to participate by, for example, attending parents' evenings and several said during the interviews that they always asked how they could help as parents but this did not prevent many of them being told, at the time of exam entry, that their child was not considered eligible to be entered for a higher tiered examination. Some of the parents in the group at the time were unaware that there *were* different tiers.

Another example of the underlying implications of associated educational matters was revealed in a workshop session by a Black careers adviser. Using examples that some were unaware of, she demonstrated how the examinations one took had a direct influence on the career options later on and a great deal of care was needed at this stage of selecting courses.

Supporting the need to know: Black history and culture – 'They have to know about their roots'

Whilst there was a high proportion of parents requesting support over the academic progress of their children, another key issue concerned the transmission of knowledge about Black history and culture; or, as the following parent describes, knowing about 'their roots'. 'I want them to be the best they can in every situation but in order for them to be positive citizens they have to know about their roots.' It was considered important for 'especially Black parents' to have this knowledge to pass on to their children because

> It's difficult for Black children growing up because the things that are projected about Black people on the whole are negative and when you fit into a European perspective of who you're supposed to be that creates problems ... you're supposed to be failing.

Different views were expressed about the best means of encouraging this as well as whose role it was to develop cultural pride and knowledge. Some were concerned that the school curriculum did not include issues of Black history and culture. Other parents, both Black and white, related that they had not been provided with this information by their own education and were therefore unable to pass this to their children. Certain participants acknowledged its importance and said they supplied this information at home because the school did not provide it whereas others said they preferred parents and the group to provide it. It was for this reason that the group wanted to celebrate Black History Month. In addition, at each session I brought in texts and other culturally relevant materials, and parents and children who were knowledgeable about Black history and culture expressed the desire to share their knowledge with the rest. Particularly successful methods, from the results of evaluation, were the Black History Month Family Drama Fun Days.

Why especially Black parents: culturally specific support

It seems suitable here to return to the theme of 'especially Black parents'. A letter to the organisation from 'a parent and grand-parent' who had attended a Black History Month Family Drama Fun Day celebration:

> My thanks to you for the brilliant idea of bringing the drama workshop to Actford to mark Black History month and promote the activities and and achievement of those who have worked so hard in the past to bring about justice and equality for Black people. The young audience showed extreme interest.

> I found the event very informative and enjoyable and most important, it gave the Black young audience the opportunity to recognise these individuals as role models and hopefully some incentive that they too can aspire to achieve.

Encouraging Black young person's aspirations to achieve recurred as a theme in the sessions. 'We have to prepare them so they can function in this society, racism notwithstanding.' Part of the preparation that the parents highlighted, was providing examples of 'role models'.

Supporting the need to know: Black role models

It is perhaps for this reason that, as noted by one participant after his first visit to the group: 'They see Actionaid as an additional academic tool, especially the mentoring. They were really attracted by the mentoring stystem.' The parents' own statements seemed to confirm the value they placed on having the mentors available to support their children:

> The mentoring thing is *great*. It's a really positive thing to be doing. It seems that the students are benefiting and the mentors are getting something out of it too.

While the mentoring programme was an 'academic tool' it was also, as other parents suggested, a 'cultural tool' by having, as role models, Black mentors who shared the same cultural background and who had achieved. Another position on this was offered by a trainer in her feedback from her workshop:

> Members expressed that they valued mentoring but some were unable to link this to an extension of the family as a role model, a person the child could emulate, which is obviously not visible in Actford.

Brewster's mother's comment about the first mentor that was provided via Actionaid, which she started attending on a regular basis, was 'she's really good but it would be better if it were a male person. He's surrounded by high achieving women'. Her daughter, she said, was 'doing very well, went to university and lives in London with her boyfriend'. Mrs Wambu had similarly asked for a male mentor, given that she was widowed and the boys may have found it 'useful to have a male person'.

Race: 'It's one of those issues'

The trainer, a senior social worker from London, had conducted a training session on 'Parenting Black children'. Although it was one of the topics the participants had identified that they desired as part of the training programme, it proved to be *the* most controversial. From the trainer's perspective:

> Because some of the members of the group had already unconsciously identified some of the barriers their children faced, I started to explore the topic of racism which I felt was a major stumbling block for parents and children. When I raised the topic of racism I was shocked by the ferocity of some of the members' reaction, the support from other members and the complete denial, from some, of its existence in Actford.

'We got into a bit of a wrangle about racism' was how another person described it:

> I think we should focus more on what it's about and getting Black children through the education system because we know that racism is preventing Black children from achieving, especially in a place like Actford.

The 'bit of a wrangle' about racism tended to converge on whether to focus on racism as an 'issue' or on strategies to assist their children in overcoming what the facilitator perceived as a 'barrier' in a place like Actford. From her viewpoint, coming from London, Actford was a place where racism would, to use the words of the parent above, be 'swept under the carpet'. The facilitator also explained that 'In a place like Actford, without Black people, it's even more important to be able to bring these types of issues out in the open.'

Supporting Black parents: 'We're sharing our perspective'

> We've got different perspectives and that's one of the things that the group's all about.

The 'sharing' of perspectives, of experience, 'of stories' was repeatedly articulated by the respondents, with sharing taking a variety of forms:

> I do think shared experience ... Experiences of former students, of mentors, experiences of the older folk. It's the stories. I would say that they don't get handed down stories. Mine for one, I hold my hand up here.
>
> (Parent)

> The young parents and the older parents, it's good having them together. The young parent may have maybe an eight-year-old and so they say, 'Oh there's no way my child would react if he were called a Black such and such. My child wouldn't ... Of course the child won't but when the child may at the age of 15, 16, 17.

> There are differences. What the younger one sees is what the older parent has experienced. But the time limit is different.

As described above, the sharing of experiences of different generations was an issue that the parents highlighted as valuable. I had not in the early stages, however, appreciated its significance. Those with younger children were able to learn from the types of issues being raised by others and the older parents were able to hear about some of the more contemporary issues being faced.

More generally, sharing in solving some of the problems or issues and obtaining advice from others was considered important, as the following dialogue reveals:

> Someone was saying that we could make the whole thing about mentoring. Well that's a thought but if people have other problems how would we address those and how would we provide a forum for people to bring along their problems.

It was not just sharing experience of success, or the mentors, it was the problems as well. Additionally, sharing the *process* of what the trainer and another parent described as 'overcoming barriers' was part of the support strategy. As one parent, now regarded as educated and 'successful', remarked, 'I've been there, I've been in the benefit office. I've gone to pick up my giro but we were brought up that you've got to help yourself, you've got to get on with it.' At the same time, she was able to learn from the experience of a parent whose experience highlighted how difficult she found it to just 'get on with it'.

The impact of their child hearing other voices aside from the parents was revealed by several of the parents to be considered a help. Perhaps the most potent example of this viewpoint was expressed by Clare:

> I welcome [this group] because I think I can say to him 'OK, you might not understand what I'm trying to say but perhaps you will find within the group the range of experiences that will somehow get through to you. This is why I welcome Actionaid and I really look forward to the future as part of the group.

'A helpful, kind and different environment'

The above description by a parent perhaps offers, from her perspective, one of the factors facilitating the success of the organisation. The reports from the parents indicated that they valued what was on offer and the environment in which the Actionaid sessions took place. It was a space that they could air issues of concern to them as parents of Black children. Dialect was heard on occasion and as one parent stated, 'we can even talk louder here'. She was comparing this with if the group were to meet at a school. The parents also, in their evaluations, showed appreciation of the African and Caribbean snacks that were made available at the meetings that we all, including myself, helped to cook.

A response to 'Does it make a difference that we're having the meetings within the community rather than at school?' was:

> I think you're more relaxed out of school to be honest, I do think that you get a more relaxed atmosphere, within the school you think there's a spy within the walls or tape recorders under the desk. At least you know that you can be free and just relax. I think it's a lot better having it out of school than within the school.

'I'm not saying all of them'

The absence of teachers was another reason cited for feeling 'more relaxed'.

Q. What about if schools say that they would like to be involved, how would you feel about having the teachers involved in it?
A. To be honest I'd rather the teachers weren't unless the teachers were Black. White teachers can be very, very negative. I find them very negative when it comes to Black children on the whole. I'm not saying all of

them but ... they are very negative towards Black children as a whole and when you're doing anything good they want to stamp on it. If it's a *Black* teacher, then fair enough because we're all here to help out one another and that's why I think it's very nice having university students.

In group meetings parents discussed ways they would have dealt with situations, like writing to the school instead of leaving it to the child to make repeated requests or buying commercially produced texts. My knowledge of the education system enabled me to provide information. Being a Black teacher seemed from their interaction to be viewed as being 'all here to help one another out'. This included them helping me out. For example, on relating to a parent [with deep regret] 'I'm going to have to say no to your dinner invitation ... I've got to work on another chapter of the thesis' she brought to my door a delicious meal.

One question on an evaluation sheet for training sessions was, 'How important do you think it is to have *trainers* of an African-Caribbean background?', with a score being requested from 'not at all' to 'extremely important', together with a reason. Comments for why it was important included:

> Because they know what sort of background I'm coming from
>
> (Parent)
>
> Because they would understand that the children are affected the most by institutionalised racism
>
> (Parent)
>
> Because they've got the same kind of background and culture so their parents might be the same kind of way.
>
> (Young person)

When asked what they felt the young persons' view on the subject of involving teachers would be, the parents reported – accurately, as later discussions with the students transpired – that the students would prefer not to.

Q. What about the kids, the young people. How do you think they would feel?

A. I think they would be more relaxed without the teachers, because you've got that strict discipline within the school. Yes Sir, No Sir, Yes mam, No mam. Though it's out of the school hours they still feel that they are in the school environment. You want them to be in a more open environment and to say what they want to say and with teachers around they're not going to, they are just going to clamp up and freeze.

The opportunity to have these dialogues and the openness in which the parents and the pupils expressed their views was noted by another visiting trainer: 'People come and people talk. I've been to meetings where you ask people and they don't talk.' As we saw in the heated debate about race, however, this openness in sharing 'different perspectives' had the potential to stifle potentially valuable contributions:

> That is what he [a grand-parent] was saying we can teach. It's not just old fashioned. He was arguing you know that these children are meeting their friends in school. They don't realise these white children are privileged here. They don't know it. What do we teach them. Oh no, they didn't see it that way. They saw it another way. Don't talk about racism, no.

With regard to the same person I was told that we should 'not let him go on so much. What he says is good, but he takes too long to say it'. However, as one of the respondents said, 'As long as we listen to each other and use our perspective constructively we can learn from each other'. This required effective chairpersonship. Likewise, in response to another viewpoint that teachers *should* be invited, the consensus was that if it was a specific 'invitation' that was 'OK', but 'not being part of *our* group'.

'Our group'

The changing perception between 'our' group and 'your' group was another aspect that proved to be both a facilitating and, at times, a constraining force. As a facilitating force it assisted, particularly, in the early stages of setting up the organisations. As one of our newsletters notes,

> parents share with us the steps they have taken to help their children achieve and to overcome obstacles. Other parents help in practical ways such as Brewster helping with this newsletter, transporting parents to and from meetings and telling others in the area about our important activities. We do this activity because we want to make a difference.

Parents were also asked if they wanted to assist in the running of the workshops or training sessions, or would like to recommend anyone. It was a participatory group in many respects.

However, there were incidents where some members offered views suggesting implicitly that it was viewed as a group *for* rather than *with* members.

> A good move, whether you can draw the people that really need it. There's some that need their eyes open, especially the younger parents. Once you become more established, get a leaflet, your aims and objectives. You can then get some funding.

At other times, seeming praise highlighted again the 'you' as opposed to the 'our'. 'You try to inject new ideas and test them and then you don't just sit down, you get up and organise it and people come.' The 'you' sometimes referred to 'me' and at other times to the management committee. Comparisons between data from early and later sessions drew the result that it was those members of the group who were present at the onset that were more likely to see it as a collective effort, 'our' group. Moreover, a critical moment, it appeared, was when the group moved from an informal set-up to the more formal structure of a management committee. Whilst this was a facilitating force in that it provided credibility to external sources, and indeed was practically necessary if we were to receive funding, it had a more constraining impact. There was, for example, more of an emphasis on minutes, agendas and reports of our work. This proved to be helpful in establishing evidence required of funding sources. However, it took up valuable time which would previously have been spent on organising training and workshop sessions.

The future of the organisation

Perhaps the most constraining factor was that of resources. It was not however, scarcity of finance per se that proved to have the most negative impact, it was lack of time. This included mine as a researcher as well as the parents, most of whom, as we saw, had extremely busy lives. It became increasingly evident that if the organisation were to have a sustainable future and build on its success, it would need to have the regular commitment of a member of staff with sufficient time. Although the group has been commended for its achievements with a community award, and several members have expressed admiration in relation to what has been achieved without *any* paid staff or anyone undertaking a full time position, the organisation is investigating securing the means of providing a part-time local parent to administer its work together with other members of the group. As one of the parents stated, in years to come 'I would still like to see the hall packed with parents, packed with pupils and packed with university students and just everybody just putting in what they've got to offer'.

Implications for schools

Perhaps the most profound implication for schools offered by Actionaid is to consider the extent to which their own school provides a 'helpful, kind and different environment' for Black parents in supporting their children's education.

Most helpful would be to provide information which fulfils the 'need to know'. This covers all stages of the educational process, from coursework requirements to careers advice. Some of the 'insider' professional information I was asked to provide could, ostensibly, have been provided by the school, as could the workshops designed with the parents' support of their child's academic achievement in mind. However, it would need a school prepared to answer in full and frank terms the questions posed such as 'How do they decide which exams to put the children in?' It would mean giving parents and pupils the type of careers information offered at Actionaid that would place them in a position of making choices and taking action informed by knowledge and understanding of the perceived parity of the various options and their impact on opportunities for pupils' careers or within higher education.

What schools 'need to know', as Clark and the various discussions portray, is that this type of information, provided at an early enough stage to make a difference, is important for 'especially Black parents'. Although they had different approaches toward overcoming racism, the parents knew the effects of racism both within school and, as mentioned by a parent in the previous chapter, when applying for jobs. The provision of both academic tools, such as this type of information and past exam papers, and cultural tools, like Black history and culture integrated within the curriculum, would form part of a school culture that would be welcomed by pupils and parents. The presence of Black teachers and Black university students were welcomed as role models, and seen as part of 'helping each other out'. In considering home–school relations, we cannot ignore the views of these parents that 'white teachers can be negative' and that there is a more 'relaxed' atmosphere in the community hall, preferable to meeting at schools. It is a positive sign for home–school relations, however, that teachers would be welcome for specific input. The implication may be that schools wishing to improve home–school relations may adopt some features of the environment created. Depending on the present quality of home–school interaction, those parents who so desired may also meet as a separate group, sharing cultural experiences, either inside or outside of the school premises.

Implications for community-based organisations

In describing the process of establishing Actionaid, the community-based action research parent empowerment project, we see how the group meets the needs of these parents by both providing the more generic information and catering to their situation as Black parents. Sharing strategies for race-specific issues such as supporting children in combating racism provoked controversy regarding the most appropriate way of doing so. This reminds us that Black parents, like parents generally, differ in their views on the most appropriate solutions to the experiences they face. The sharing of experience and strategies among the different age groups and circumstances was successful and facilitated progress, particularly when members shared how they had overcome obstacles. Having both parents and pupils within

Chapter 5

Mediaid: 'Let us talk'
A home–school mediation organisation

Mediaid: Mediation

Mediaid is a community-based, registered charity. Support is in the form of a home–school mediation role. Mediation types of organisation have the aim of being the middle person or 'honest broker' in a situation between the home and the school; mediation usually occurs when a problem has already been identified. The purpose, it is claimed, is not to represent either 'side' but to attempt to act neutrally and reconcile the views of the family with those of the school when there is a situation that needs to be resolved.

A brief history

The Mediaid organisation has been in operation since 2000. It was founded amidst national and local concern over the high rates of exclusion of African and Caribbean students. Indeed, its first promotional report begins with research findings from the DfEE and locally. It reveals that nationally, although Black pupils constitute only 2.5 per cent of the national school population, 10 per cent of those permanently excluded were of African and Caribbean origin and at a local level, throughout the borough in which the organisation was based, of the 78 pupils excluded that year 46 per cent were African and Caribbean.

Starting on a completely voluntary basis, the organisation was set up to intervene in this process. The report describes how they began by writing to local schools outlining the way in which their support and counselling of pupils at risk of exclusion may complement the role of the school. Their initial end-of-year figures reveal that they worked with fifteen pupils from three schools and their next year's report shows that this expanded to thirty-five pupils from nine schools. These figures have since increased considerably and the organisation now covers schools and colleges in surrounding boroughs. They have developed a wider range of preventative and intervention strategies for the families. In conjunction with this increase, their completely voluntary status has moved to a more diversified funding base. While the contribution from the LEA started with a small administration grant and support 'in kind' of similarly small accommodation, at a finalising interview I was shown that a downstairs office had been given over to the group to augment their upstairs area and I was informed that they now had increased funding from the LEA, individual schools and a number of national and local agencies.

A rationale

Exclusions were initially the core concern within the rationale for the setting up of the group. It is stated for example that 'The Black community and parents of Black children fear that these exclusions will inevitably lead to the destruction of their children's ability to perform and most probably turn them into liabilities to the community.' Supporting Black parents is intended to assuage the tide of exclusions and the concerns of the parents about not only its detrimental effect on the attainment of their own children but also the negative effect this may have on the Black community and culture as a whole. Group and individual discussions with the staff underscore their consistent view that they cannot intervene in this cycle without a three-pronged strategy of working with parents, children and schools. Cultural factors in relation to exclusions are a key part of their rationale. 'Cultural bridge building' was a central strategy for their intervention in this process in order to try to enable teachers to better understand the culture of Black families. In interviews, they discuss common cultural stereotypes they have observed in teachers; for example, that Black children appear louder than their white counterparts. Their perspective is that by supporting the teachers to better understand Black pupils they are supporting the parents, as this strategy has the potential of preventing exclusions based on cultural misunderstanding. Their message to schools and teachers is, therefore, 'we are open, the pupils you are concerned about are here, come and let us talk and see what solutions we can arrive at'. Their policy was, at the time, an explicit one of 'non-confrontation'. This stance is contrasted by one of the staff with another local organisation working with Black families: 'There is an organisation in this borough that does that. It's more political than *we* are.'

Upon being asked to explain this, the member of staff was quite clear that there was sometimes a need for a more 'political' stance and at the same time was adamant that it was not going to be provided by them:

> What we're trying to do now is to try and start networking rather than saying that she is this and we are that, she is left wing and we are right wing ... and all that nonsense. If we know that she's good in a particular area we can pass someone on. We are trying to employ strategies. If it comes to it, we can get someone else to do it. What it boils down to is

that we're here to support young people and if they can do a better job then let them do it.

The member of staff explained that by 'politics' he was referring to 'party politics'. He believed that the leader of the organisation he was referring to had more of what he described as 'political clout' than their organisation because of her involvement with party politics. Notwithstanding, her position was not considered 'sensible' for them.

One of the complexities was that things seemed to change substantially over quite a short period. During the main phase of the research, the common stance taken by the members of the organisation was the apolitical one described above, but at a final interview with a spokesperson for the organisation a year later a radical change in stance had seemingly occurred.

Interviews with key staff and some parents at the advocacy organisation, who had initially sought support from the mediation service and some documentary material, do point to the aforementioned 'non-confrontational' approach. The reasoning behind this, according to an interview response from one of the volunteers, is that 'the system does not allow for confrontation'. If a child is up for exclusion therefore their stance would be, at the time, to try to point out to the head teacher that they do not wish to undermine any professional judgement but would implore them to take previous good character into account and decide on a lesser punishment than permanent exclusion. As part of the negotiation process they would stress their input into working with the child and the family if the head teacher were to reconsider.

Analysis suggests that the organisation did not place as much emphasis on this part of their work as on the more preventative strategies. They were, as a volunteer explained:

> Trying to educate them [the parents] to understand what the school system is like. It's difficult really for them to know the school system ... and the way we approach things [referring to Black parents]. They always think that our parents are confrontational.

Explicitly, Mediaid seeks to ensure that they are not perceived as being confrontational. Instead, they adopt a range of strategies working with the parents, child and school. In this reporting of the findings, however, I will naturally, given the nature of this investigation, concentrate on their work with families in terms of supporting them to support their children's education. However, as the following diagram demonstrates, their activities are intentionally linked so as to impact on one another for the benefit of the child, who is at the centre of the organisation's work. This is expressed in an extract on the wall of the organisation, which, as one volunteer explained, describes its ethos: 'Every child has natural capabilities. Given the right encouragement these can be developed.'

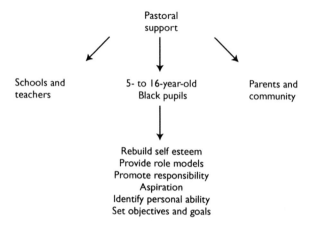

Figure 5.1 Mediaid's approach to the support of Black parents and their families (taken from a publicity brochure of the organisation)

The nature of the support on offer to families

The multi-pronged approach to the support of Black parents and their families is represented diagrammatically above.

Pastoral support

The organisation assists the family by providing pastoral support both at home and within the school. Home-based support takes the form of mentors visiting the family of a child who has been referred to the organisation, usually by a school. Before mentoring can take place it is a requirement of the organisation that the parent is also involved and the parent signs an undertaking to this effect. During the home visits the intention, according to the publicity document is 'to discuss the situation, problems and possible solutions'.

Support to families: some cases

Duane's family

I was able to observe a home visit pastoral session with a boy who was perceived by the school as 'having disciplinary problems' for a variety of reasons. During this observation, taking place at around 7 p.m., it was noted that the time the pastoral support worker, Perry, had with the mother was quite brief as she was getting ready to go to work on her night shift as a nurse. She appeared, from her brief conversation with the pastoral support worker, to lead quite a hectic life style, juggling her work with being a single parent of boys. This aspect of the life of some Black parents is recognised within Mediaid's literature:

Mediaid recognises the circumstances and problems of black workers. Of that client group that it has been able to help, Mediaid has noted that some parents are absent in the evening; many single parents try to hold down several low paid jobs to support the family.

(Mediaid brochure, section 8.9)

It seemed from the warmth of her reception that Duane's mother welcomed Perry's assistance and she willingly trusted him to embark on a discussion with her son while she went upstairs to change into her nurses' uniform. Her leaving may, however, have been a deliberate ploy. An earlier interview with the support worker during the day had indicated that one of the problems he finds with the organisation is that visits often occur in front of the parents and sometimes the children do not say very much under these circumstances.

Duane did not at first appear to be very communicative without his mother's presence. This could, of course, have been because of my being there. However, I soon observed how effective the pastoral support volunteer was at drawing him out and encouraging him to speak; the subject of their discussion became far ranging. In attempting to analyse a focus to their discussion it seems that Duane was being encouraged to consider some short and medium term goals and to use his time effectively in an effort to realise them. Instead, he seemed, from his comments to Perry, to spend a lot of time watching videos. He asked Perry, 'Can't you see me more regularly, I'm bored.' Once a fortnight was the usual policy of the organisation but he was attempting to persuade Perry to organise group trips out for young people during the forthcoming holiday. 'Friends' may have been a source of problems for the young man. He was articulating, for example, 'The people you think are your real friends always end up doing something stupid … If the police catch you …' The 'friendship' theme extended to his girlfriend and the fact that she was still at school so he 'didn't pay her much attention'. Missing from the conversation was any direct reference to his own school or schoolwork. He did mention that he had applied for a part-time job at a local supermarket and was waiting to hear from them. In considering the nature of the support offered in such interaction it would seem to lay in Perry offering guidance in a 'softly softly' manner in a spirit of male camaraderie.

Teresa's family

A different type of home-based pastoral support was observed when I accompanied Perry and Yvonne, a female mentor, to visit a mother, Julia, and her daughter, Teresa, 14, who had been permanently excluded. Her mother had approached the organisation for assistance in appealing against the decision to exclude and had since changed her mind and was seeking their help in finding a school to take Teresa. This was the intended focus of the visit.

At this session it was noted that Perry and Yvonne undertook differentiated roles in terms of pastoral support. First, they had a discussion with both mother and child then Yvonne stayed in one room talking with the daughter, Teresa, while Perry accompanied the mother, Julia. A complex range of educational and social factors was elicited from the results of analysis of the meeting. Educationally, the dominant theme was how very difficult it was to obtain a place in a school once a child had been excluded, with issues surrounding the exclusion process from the perspective of the family and the school.

From Teresa's point of view, the immediate process leading to exclusion was that 'a girl got beaten up by some of [her] friends'. She was *there,* she said, and the next day she was 'suspended' because she 'didn't do anything to stop it'. She seemed to believe it very unfair that the person who did start the fight was not excluded. Teresa considered that her exclusion was because she had one fight before and had been 'suspended' and placed under 'contract' but the other pupils had not previously been suspended. She also pointed out that she 'didn't get on' with her form teacher and one subject teacher. She reported quite passionately '*Every* science lesson I was sent out.' She said she was always 'in dispute' with her form teacher and that when the head teacher became involved he would 'exaggerate'. Her understanding was that 'It got to him because I stood up to him.'

Her mother, in turn, believed that 'some of these Black parents are scared to speak up to him [the head teacher] and that's what the problem is'. Some of the issues she mentioned that she had 'spoken up' about included that the head teacher had reported that he had sent her a letter but was not able to find a copy of the letter on file. Moreover, at the time he wished to exclude Teresa he 'suddenly brought up twenty-two incidents'. The letter she produced that he had written included:

> If a member of staff talks with Teresa she is abusive, rude and defiant (see conduct log). I am afraid that we as a school have had enough. As I have said I am excluding her from the school in an effort to protect other pupils and my staff. As you know I do not take this decision lightly and in haste. I believe that we as a school and indeed you as her mother have been more than patient with her.

The 'conduct' referred to a Maths teacher describing Teresa's attitude, her 'body language' and 'frowning.' Her mother admitted that 'Teresa is not innocent' and that she 'likes to be in the limelight'. She did, however, believe that her reputation had come with her from her school in Leicester and that she was never going to shake off that reputation. Moreover, having been on a 'contract' 'all eyes would be on Teresa'. During the interview she also pointed out Teresa's intelligence and that she had been placed in the higher sets.

From Julia's perspective, she had been supportive of the school. 'As soon as they wrote me a letter I phone up.' Yet, her view seemed to be that the school was 'always trying to find out' what she referred to as her 'business'. This included, she said, things like whether she was a single parent. She was 'not impressed by the school's dealing with Black parents and children' and gave examples of their use of language like 'coloured' people and a letter she had been shown from another parent where the head had 'written a letter to a mixed race girl calling her names'. Teresa's mother had eventually decided not to appeal as, in her statement, 'I haven't got the strength to argue with them.'

At the time of the home visit, Teresa was receiving home tuition for 'a few hours' a week, funded by the LEA. They had been informed that was the only academic support available, apart from a place at a Pupil Referral Unit. The mother did not wish her daughter to attend the PRU. Perry was in the process of asking the mother what school she wanted while Yvonne was asking Teresa. It was soon revealed that the impact of the exclusion was that Teresa had missed her SATS. She would also, of course, have to find a school willing to take her. Given the difficulty I was aware that Perry was experiencing in this direction, related in a pre-visit discussion, my field notes recorded his patience when, having taken on board Teresa's preference not to attend a girls' school, she dismissed one of his suggestions on the basis of its 'old fashioned' uniform. The school she was dismissing was, from my knowledge of the area, a multicultural school, relatively high achieving with a fairly 'relaxed' ethos, and Perry or his Chairman would have needed to use influence with 'contacts' at the school in order for her to be accepted.

Pablo and his son

The support on this occasion took place in the office. The data arise from observation of the interaction of two of the personnel, Perry and Ajani, with a father of two, Pablo, who had visited the office for support, together with a subsequent group interview of the father and two workers from Mediaid. During the course of the interview, he explained that the 'problems' were to do with his fourteen-year-old son, Dominic. He also, he said, had a fifteen-year-old girl at the same school, who was 'fine, having no problems'. His son, in contrast, has 'daily problems'. He put this down to their gender:

A year apart, the same school, they have some of the same teachers, and yet the treatment of my daughter compared to my son ... when you sit down to parents' evenings you can *feel* it. The whole *manner* changes. I thought it wouldn't happen because you know, the same school, the same family.

In some respects the girls are treated slightly differently to the ways boys are treated. I would say almost from *nursery* class stage. Right through to examination level and then leaving school. The boys are almost *expected* to fail.

In explaining the situation, he cited the attitude of the teachers as an issue: 'They're not supportive' was an initial comment, which was expanded to:

He [his son] feels that they don't acknowledge certain things. If there's something that he doesn't understand or something he needs help with, they just leave him to it. He doesn't always get into any *trouble*, they just don't acknowledge him. Which to me means that they're failing him as a student.

Perry and Ajani, in their efforts to support him, asked whether he had brought this to the attention of the school. His response was, 'In an effort not to aggravate the situation I don't bring this observation to the front.' He had, however, been to the form tutor and the Head of Year. He went to parents' evenings regularly but believed 'they tell you what they suspect you want to hear'. This was reinforced with a comment later on that, 'I think the problem with school in general is a lack of fruitful communication'. He would have liked, he said, to have 'got him a private tutor' but 'couldn't afford it'. He also discussed how, when he went to the PTA, he 'was the lone Black parent'. In relation to school-based sessions for involvement, one of the issues that emerged was that, from his perspective:

You're looked on, you're judged, by the way you dress, the way you speak and as a consequence of that your child now is judged. If the parent doesn't look tidy they think the child can't *think* straight. It's a misconception but that's how schools are generally.

When you go to parents' evening you look around and you'll notice that the parents that are there ... the Black parents, are usually dressed casually. The white parents are usually dressed as though they've just come from work ... On the occasions that I've noticed Black parents there in their shirts and ties they've been treated differently to the rest of us.

On probing, other issues came to the fore: some related to his son, others to the school. A Saturday supplementary school was suggested but his son 'didn't want to go to Saturday school' and although his father said he could teach him, he spoke of his son's 'pride' preventing him. Some gender issues related to Black boys were revealed:

One of the problems our youth encounter is the way they're seen by their peers and then by the outside world. Our youth are sensitive, and a Black man won't show that he's sensitive, they pick up on things so quickly.

He also explained that his son has 'a distinct lack of confidence ... but is not going to admit it to everyone, no *absolutely* not'. This, he believed, 'comes back to society and their expectations about Black men'. Ajani, the older Black man, empathised, saying, 'It is called a mask. A lot of Black men you see are wearing a *mask* and the mask is there for you not to see that they haven't got any confidence.' Pablo responded by explaining how he started on a teaching course but stopped and never resumed.

I think with encouragement, I could do it. I could certainly get through the learning side of teaching. But I feel I need to be exemplary, I might be articulate but I need more than that and if I don't *have* more than that, then I don't feel confident. I feel I've got to start achieving before I can start inspiring young children, inspiring my son.

His son, he expressed the belief, preferred to communicate with him on aspects unrelated to school:

We have the kind of relationship that those things to do with school she tends not to tell me but like his recreation he would. He would tell me about the basketball and football and he tells me about the girls ... Black and white ... who accost him on his way home. He'll tell me about that but not his school work.

What he wanted for his son's education, he said, was:

For him to at least emerge from school, with a basic grounding in English, mathematics and perhaps three other subjects ... at least average grades in those subjects ... perhaps IT.

In connection with his expectations of the school, he stated, 'I expect them to identify the areas where he's needing improving and then if they don't have the resources to bring about an improvement in that area to let *me* know so that I can compensate.' Seeking the support of Mediaid was part of that process. He wasn't, he said, satisfied with his relationship with Dominic's school: 'They will communicate with me, *yes*, but in a negative way. By and large when I speak to staff it's because of an occurrence and usually that occurrence is negative so I feel that nothing positive is happening.'

Ajani explained to the parent that, as part of their support to parents, Mediaid 'can go in and talk to teachers and see how we can resolve matters'. Pablo seemed more interested in the idea of the parents' forum:

It's a collective strength, it's an old adage, united we stand, divided we fall ... It's one thing to have communication between schools and parents but it's also important that we have communication between each other because then you build community.

'Where do we turn?'

The above question, from Pablo, provided a poignant plea for support for Black parents:

As far as our children and parents are concerned they need support, support from knowledgeable people. People who will understand how schools work. So when education fails us and society fails us, when our *parents* fail us because they can't understand what's *happening* in society, where do we *turn*? If there's an organisation that takes account of that ... and can actually do something about it.

Parent-related aspects of Mediaid's work

Exclusions

According to the Chairman, David, 'the parents wanted training about exclusions. They did not understand the law and needed information about the basic legal process'. The video I was provided with was Mediaid's response to this need. It was very factual, outlining the processes in a clear manner. David told me that the LEA had helped to finance it, had bought many copies and it was being used for training governors and others at the LEA and beyond.

The video was presented by Ade, a barrister of African ancestry. I was not able to meet with him but was provided by David with the information that Mediaid had enlisted his services due to increasing requests for assistance over exclusions. This aspect of Mediaid's support for parents was therefore not present during the main phase of the research but was reported during the final interview, a year later. David explained that the barrister, with expertise in educational law, meets with the parent and the child, then goes through the case with the parent. His strategy, it was said, was to analyse from the evidence what that school should have been doing and where they had failed to meet their legal duties. An example was where a school had failed to meet its statutory requirements to provide support over the special educational needs of a boy. According to the volunteer pastoral support worker, discussing the needs of children in general, not just those categorised as having special educational needs:

What we find in the majority of cases the schools don't actually do that. They're quite happy to let the child carry on doing their old behaviour. They give no support in helping that child so that's how we win the majority of the cases.

The Chairman spoke of a 'tangible increase in their achievement' in appealing against the decision of a school to exclude since using the services of the trained barrister. The figures were revealed in an interview with Perry:

We've had thirteen of our clients excluded permanently and on appeal we've won ten of them and of the other three we won one at the disciplinary governors' appeal so we won eleven of the thirteen appeals. Compared to the national average our one is great.

This figure was validated in their most recent report. The quantitative evidence proved especially useful since at the time of the main phase of the research, the opportunities had not been available to interview the parents to the extent of the opportunities at Advocaid.

Pastoral support: the parents' culture

Apart from the home visits and the observations in the office, further information about Mediaid's work with parents was gleaned from interviews with the staff. 'We need to actually understand our roots and culture' was mentioned by Perry as an important factor in supporting Black families. As part of the pastoral and mentoring support to the family the pastoral team leader related that he attempts to encourage the parents to inform their children about their cultural background. Even for the children born in this country he believed 'it is important for the child to know about where the parents are from'. Therefore, he says, when speaking to the young person he will ask them questions about where their parents are from, and to give him information about the parents' home country, for example, the things they do over there and what the country is good for. 'I try to get the parents to talk to their children about their upbringing ... we need to be looking at our parents' parents ... how many children will know about their parents' parents?'

A Parents' Forum

During the fieldwork, it was explained that the organisation was planning to set up a Parents' Forum. The forum had, I was informed, 'been launched but was not yet fully operational'. An initial document states Mediaid's intention 'to create a forum where parents, teachers and pupils will freely interact to help resolve contentious issues'. In interviews with the

Chairman, the pastoral support worker and other volunteers, the presence of teachers is not mentioned. Instead, the philosophy behind the setting up of such a forum seems to be one whereby the parents would meet together and support each other under the guidance of a facilitator provided by the organisation. The emphasis here was on working collectively with parents in addition to Mediaid's work with individual families in their home.

Other work carried out by Mediaid

School-based pastoral support

During the course of an interview, Perry discussed the school-based pastoral support for students. 'For me, it works a lot better in the sense that we can see more people ... if schools will allow us to take the young people out of lesson and do the group work.'

> We talk about communication, we talk about the media, how the media portrays us, we talk about feelings and emotions, we talk about the image that you portray to people and the image that you'd *like* to portray to people, we talk about relationships and drugs.

Many, if not most, of the young people taking part in these group discussions were, said Perry, Black boys and in his view they 'enjoyed the opportunity of taking part in these types of discussions in a group setting'. He also believed that, 'it was providing the boys, the young people, with a general range of communication and interpersonal skills, useful both academically and socially'. Matters considered important to adolescents in general and Black youngsters in particular could be discussed with another Black man, who was not a teacher or parent. Direct evidence of Perry conducting these sessions could not be collected. I was told that most of the group of Black boys had been referred to the organisation because in the view of the school they were causing behavioural difficulties, underachieving or were at risk of exclusion.

The Saturday project: community-based academic and cultural support

During the main phase of the fieldwork I was informed that a 'Saturday project' was being set up. This was described as a 'preventative measure to support the academic and social side of the young person's development'. They were keen to inform me they wanted the activities to be viewed as different from attending school, therefore they 'did not call it a Saturday school but a Saturday project'. It 'developed from an emphasis on KS2 to KS4 Maths and English and some Black history'. Such provision was considered to be supporting the aims of Black families and the Black community for their children's academic success. The aim was to have an environment that was fun but also conducive to learning. Given the limitations of time and the decision to focus on those activities directly related to parent/family support such as the pastoral visits, I was unable to visit the Saturday school. I was told by Perry, however, that after some initial problems, a year after its inception, the project was 'showing success'.

Key themes and issues

Several issues proved key in relation to the research questions on how the organisations supported parents. The first to be reported is that of parental support, social class and socio-personal circumstances.

Parental support: race and social class

One new aspect of the work of the organisation was its contract with the local Youth Offending Team. In informing me about this development, after the main phase of the fieldwork, the Chairman described the role of Mediaid as 'the provision of support to parents who had been before the Court system on behalf of their child and received a "Parents' Order". It was part of new government policy to 'help the parent help the child so that the child does not re-offend'. According to the Chairman, all the referrals from the Youth Offending Team had been white parents. The Chairman informed me during the interview that 40 per cent of the parents were white.

This was a rather unexpected finding. During the entire phase of the fieldwork the key emphasis of the documentary, interview and observation evidence was on intervention work with Black families, in particular those of African and Caribbean ancestry. All the team members I had met on their visits to the office shared this ancestry and a re-examination of the data from that time did not reveal the intention to expand the delivery of their services beyond Black parents.

The new stance taken by the Chairman was, in his words, 'a parent is a parent is a parent' and their work with parents and in the Parents' Forum was being delivered in this light. In order to probe this aspect I asked his opinions as to whether the needs of Black parents differed from the needs of parents in general. His response was:

> I would say that the needs are converging. As Black parents live longer in this country their needs are converging with the white parents in this country. For those who have just *arrived* the gap is still very wide. For example when we're dealing with refugees ... from Somalia. Their needs are different, but for parents who are born here and their children

are having problems at school their needs, their mentality, their attitudes, are not far from white working-class parents.

Throughout his explanation there was no reference to race, racism or cultural needs. In contrast, re-analysis of their documentary material revealed that they frequently used terms such as African and Caribbean, culture and Black people and whilst my analysis found no mention of the word racism, their brochure states quite categorically: '**Most of Mediaid's clients are from low income single parent families. Acknowledgement of these facts does not nullify, however, the important fact that cultural difference and racial disadvantage are also central to the exclusion of black pupils.**' (The emboldenment is that of Mediaid, indicative of intention to emphasise.)

Rather than a racial dimension, the Chairman seemed from the above interview to consider class or their 'low income' as a predominant factor. He expands on this by saying that 'if you look at some of our clients who really *are* struggling, their behavioural patterns and their needs and support requirements are not that far from the white working-class parents'. Initially, in the Chairman's interview, he suggested that 'Black' is being referred in a homogenised manner in terms of social class, one which is equivalent to the white working class. Later, however, he appeared to contradict this view by stating: 'Within the Black community there is a middle class who will do exactly what the white parents do. Complain about everything, write about everything, insist on the child being given its rights.' It is the white middle class as opposed to the previous distinct mention of the white working class that appears to be being referred to here. According to him it is the middle classes who have been availing themselves of their newly formed Saturday project providing academic support, even though it was not set up for them. This is because 'they take advantage of everything that's going on for the child'.

An attempt was made to follow the above themes, through another interview with Perry, the pastoral support volunteer. Perry agreed that 'a parent is a parent is a parent' but believed that Black parents 'bring their children up differently from white people'. In his experience, 'Afro Caribbeans they teach their children long before they actually go to school'. Whereas, he says, 'they teach aspects such as a, b, c and number'. He contrasts this with his perception of white [working-class] parents who, he said, 'seem to bring up their children gaa gaa goo goo, gaa gaa goo goo'. This he believes has an adverse effect on the Black child when he starts school. 'What happens is when those children start school, the teachers are geared to teaching those white kids who haven't been taught a, b, c, d, e, who haven't been taught that two and two is four.' As a result, the Black child gets restless and starts 'messing around'.

Lone parents and child development: an emergent issue

In discussing their work with parents, comparisons across a number of interviews with the volunteers confirmed the documentary statement that most (but not all) of the parents seeking their support were from single parent households. The interviews revealed that this included the White community. An extract from an interview with a volunteer states 'I'm not going to stereotype but two parents will bring up their child different from one.'

He went on, however, to explain how being a 'single parent' may not necessarily lead to negative effects on a child's development:

> Because they're single parents they will talk to their children as if they're semi talking to an adult because they need that adult stimulation so that for a child to be at home and have your parent talking to you like an adult and you have some teacher talking to you like a *kid* you think what's going on here. What're you talking to me like that for. I'm no fool. So the children, they're saying the teachers 'aint talking to them with *respect*. They're not talking to them like an adult which their parents are doing.

This belief, he explained, was based on experience of home visits by himself and others, noting interaction with single parents and their child as well as being able to work with the child at school.

Gender and supporting parents: an emergent theme

Another theme emerging from my analysis was the impact of gender on the nature of support required by Black families. Issues about the impact of supporting Black mothers in supporting their male children were cited in interviews with both the male and female pastoral worker. Data from the organisation's reports revealed that most of the pupils referred to the organisation were boys and that, in common with the national statistics, the exclusion rate for Black boys was higher than that of Black girls. Three of the organisation's staff informed me that schools had made urgent requests for more male mentors. Pablo's case revealed instances of where he believed his son and daughter were treated differently. At the same time, cases such as Teresa above demonstrate the impact of involvement with female mentors.

Organisational features

A distinctive feature of this organisation was the rapid development of its activities between the time when I first made contact with the organisation and my final interviews a year later. These activities seem to have been multiple and fundamental and, to a great extent, due to the Chairman, David.

His demographic profile included experience as a successful businessman, a doctorate and a governor of a higher educational institute. He was not from the local area in the way some of the volunteers were. The Chairman seemed to have the dominant role in the organisation, explaining his position as 'like a Chief Executive'. David's view was that 'to achieve success it is necessary to have strategies to secure a sound financial footing'. According to him, 'one of the reasons so many organisations fold is that they are too reliant on grants'. Instead, he said it was 'better to secure contracts'. The financial developments were many. He explained that he had secured a contract with the Youth Offending Team. Two-year renewable contracts for support and training had been entered into with a number of local and adjacent schools and colleges. The financial and general support of schools, the LEA and key agencies is viewed by him as being 'crucial to success', especially as most of its referrals come from schools. As he reported in an interview, 'The schools know what we are doing. They are comfortable buying services for us to use within the school environment.' Perry, the pastoral team leader, related how 'The Metropolitan Police heard that we were setting up the Parents' Forum and said, to help you along, we will donate ten thousand pounds so you can actually employ someone to work with the parents.' On being asked directly whether there is potential for conflicts of interests in obtaining financial and other support the Chairman denied this emphatically:

> No, we do not ever foresee a time when confrontation is of any use to the child's education. Even if we've got a contract helping a school and the school is obviously 'abusing' the child we will take the case up. That is clear in the contract. We hope that in most cases, because we are part of the school, we are able to bring the issue to light.

Partnership: some issues

As an illustration of the partnership approach to schools, Mediaid includes in its latest brochure the following endorsement from a local head teacher: 'Mediaid is one of the only support agencies which is totally non discriminatory – They will help anyone. They provide support in an integrated, not a segregated fashion, without producing any barriers.'

One of the volunteers did, however, consider as a barrier to their work that 'Some schools have used us. They've called us in for support, excluded the child and said, oh we had Mediaid working for us when it came to appeal.' Another called the partnership 'a con'.

> A school will ring us up and say we've got a child who's in danger of being excluded. Can you go and see him, so we go round to his parents' house, we speak to his parents and to him. In the meantime, the school

still has a problem with this child. If the child gets excluded from the school it looks like we've failed, it looks like we *as an organisation* have failed. It's a big con. I don't like the way it works.

According to the organisation's brochure, 'Mediaid's most significant achievement to date has been its role as a bridge builder between schools and parents'. The Chairman, however, did not appear to consider the possibility of the type of tensions inherent in this concept that some of the pastoral support workers articulated. Instead, he explained how partnerships with the LEA had enabled the volunteers to be provided with a ten-week training course by the Council. In the perspective of the Chairman, the ability to forge successful partnerships has been important to the success of the organisation. Again, its most recent brochure contains approbatory statements from the Director of Education and the Chief Superintendent of the Metropolitan Police.

Exclusions: a change of strategies – a new impact

The 'softly softly' position described by the staff and the 'pleading' reported by the two parents I met through Advocaid, who had interpreted this as 'being 'more on the side of the school', appeared to have shifted dramatically. The increased impact in the area of supporting parents over exclusions is indicated in the increase in the number of cases won on appeal. This impact may, however, be diminished by changes in the law. According to Perry, the new laws mean that cases they had won they now 'would have lost since schools now have more power to exclude'. He also described how 'now the video has been made, we have to change things and update it for the parents'.

'The commitment of the volunteers'

A primary reason for the success of Mediaid, said the Chairman, was 'the commitment of the volunteers'. He cited, for example, 'Perry has been there for two years, he has not been paid a salary. It's a long time in a young man's life not to be paid a salary.' He pointed out, however, that Perry was reimbursed for his expenses. Whilst in the field I observed a commitment to the job indicated by long hours in the office, followed by home visits. Similarly, Perry acted upon the concerns of Duane, discussed earlier, by initiating activities in the summer break for young people. Evidence of the appreciation of the pupils was observed when I visited on one of the days he was just about to take them out. His support for Black families, especially the Black boys and Black fathers with whom I saw him interacting, was apparent in that he appeared keen for them to succeed, to have high ambitions and was enthusiastic in the expressions of his desire to support them toward this. In addition, observations revealed him as not being patronising in this support and having a realistic sense of the environmental and other factors which might impinge on their success. As a local young Black Rastafarian man, dreadlocked, with a 'South London' accent, he appeared to convey 'street credibility' combined with a sense of purpose. Observations also revealed that the young people, mentors and the parents I observed him with seemed able to relate to him. Similarly, Yvonne, the young Black female mentor who accompanied him on the home visits, appeared to be able to develop a rapport with Teresa and with her mother. The organisation's ability to recruit and retain a range of suitable Black volunteers as mentors, trainers and administrators contributes to the successful delivery of the services to Black families. However, the Chairman himself expressed concern as to how long the organisation would be able to rely on their goodwill and commitment. He explained that Mediaid was attempting to secure funding to finance Perry's post. He seemed keen to keep men like Perry within the organisation, seemingly aware that the trust engendered by Perry and others like him, as indicated above, was crucial to the survival of Mediaid in building bridges to the wider Black community.

Implications and recommendations for schools

The testimonies of the parents import useful advice for schools. Like the parents at Actionaid, for Pablo, as a dedicated father, 'fruitful' communication focusing on identifying his son's learning needs and the respective role of the school and himself in meeting those needs would lead to a significant improvement in his relations with the school and potentially in his son's achievement. A key learning point is that the school is clearly unaware of Pablo's skills and attributes and indeed of the way in which they could have supported him in his efforts to become a teacher. The potential impact of such knowledge is lost.

Similarly, schools 'need to know' if a child is being sent out of a particular lesson in every lesson of that class in order to address the situation.

A system of regular classroom observations at middle or senior leadership level has the potential to uncover the situation in Teresa's case. Systematic classroom observations, pupil tracking and constructive use of data may also enable the school to become aware of teachers and tutors who are successful in raising attainment across the cultural spectrum and, conversely, those who may benefit from support and further training in this area or in the area of the teacher's role in promoting behaviour for learning or indeed those teachers who may themselves be displaying inappropriate behaviour in classrooms.

Teresa's 'abusive, rude and defiant' behaviour is clearly a challenge. A consistent approach with clear behavioural boundaries and expectations across the school is likely to lead to fewer 'disputes' and improved behaviour, especially if this is done at the onset, perhaps immediately on her arrival at the school, rather than when the school has 'had enough'. Complementary strategies may include appropriate inter-agency support for the root cause of such behaviour, the move to London, for example, and the above focus on 'behaviour for learning' perhaps provided by a Learning Mentor. This is likely to be helpful to all concerned, to improve behaviour and reduce exclusions. In contrast, bringing up numerous incidents at the point of exclusion is poor practice and one would question why the parent is only asked to see the conduct log at this stage. As an effort to 'protect other pupils and my staff' is a basis for exclusion that is commonly cited by head teachers. It can, however, cover a whole spectrum of behaviour, from fights to verbal abuse. If a school is to be seen to be fair in its decisions to exclude, it is necessary to provide clarity and adherence to agreed policies, and to demonstrate that an exclusion is not differentially used for pupils with similar offences.

Gender differences are revealed through Mediaid. Teresa's case suggests that a system of monitoring and evaluation of policies and practice, if it included a gender component, may act as a preventative measure in alerting staff to the potential for girls to slip back or a pattern where 'boys are expected to fail' and girls and boys, as Pablo suggests, are treated differently but with a similar negative outcome for their learning. Pastoral and academic systems of support for pupils would therefore include attention to girls as well as boys who may be at risk of underachieving. The situations depicted in the case studies suggest that the fact that a child has ability, as indicated by being placed in higher sets, appears to have been buried beneath behavioural issues. Conversely, Pablo's son is 'unacknowledged' as long as he does not exhibit overt displays of misbehaviour. Meanwhile, his learning needs are unmet.

Basic advice about the use of culturally appropriate terminology arises from Teresa's case. For many in the Black community, like Teresa's mother (and included in the Macpherson report), the use of 'coloured people' suggests a lack of cultural knowledge and understanding, as this phrase is outmoded and viewed by many, including Teresa's family, as offensive to the point of seeming racist. Proactively seeking the support of organisations like Mediaid in a long-term programme of cultural bridge-building, working with schools, parents and pupils, including work on resolving 'disputes' in a 'non-confrontational' manner, is likely to reap benefits in supporting Black pupils, parents and schools.

Implications for the support organisation

This relatively new support organisation is largely successful in its attempts to 'build cultural bridges' between the parent, child and school by working with all three. It attempts to increase understanding of each other, prevent exclusions and, where the child has been excluded, to intervene in a 'softly softly' manner, at least initially.

Observations of their pastoral work at the homes of families revealed many expressions of appreciation of the pastoral input of the support workers. It is the pastoral support that, in the views of the parents, seemed to most meet their needs. The advice and information about schools and contacts with educational institutions were also of benefit to parents, like Teresa's mother, who needed to find a school for their child. Teresa's mother had not however had the benefit of preventative measures since the organisation was only contacted at the stage when the family was considering appealing against the school's decision to exclude. This portrays how important it is for such organisations to be involved at a stage early enough to use their preventative strategy and certainly not at the stage where exclusion appears inevitable or where the organisations feel they have been used as a 'con'.

The home visits with Teresa and her mother showed also that the family was willing to discuss the way in which domestic and personal circumstances had impinged on their relationship, and on Teresa's education, in a way that they were unwilling to discuss with the school, where they felt the school was intruding on their 'business'. The female pastoral workers seemed to be having an important role in attempting to rebuild the relationship between Teresa and her mother and analysis showed that it is with this worker that Teresa displayed her best behaviour.

The success of Mediaid in forging partnerships with schools and other agencies has led to the award of contracts. These include a contract with the Youth Offenders Team and finance obtained from the police. There are important implications here for organisations wishing to 'secure a sound financial footing' yet maintain a degree of independence in how they deliver support. One of the conditions of their financial decisions is that their clients extend to other ethnic groups. Some of their partnership arrangements may have created caution in their core client group, in this instance Black parents.

Perry shows in-depth understanding of cultural issues including the more constructive features of the parenting style of Black lone parents and the importance of parents passing to their children understanding of their own upbringing and cultural heritage. His analysis of whether 'a parent is a parent is a parent' portrays incisively the relative impact of class, culture and race on parental support needs.

The knowledge and commitment of Perry, as a Black male volunteer is key to the success of Mediaid and highlights the need for organisations to recruit more such volunteers. In doing this, organisations providing support to schools and families may be successful in working with schools and the pupils to prevent boys from becoming part of the national statistics of underachievement and high exclusions of Black boys. It is significant in this respect that schools urgently sought more Black male mentors from the organisation and that the mother Perry was working with was the mother of two Black boys. Perry was able to meet the school's request, Perry's mother appreciated his input, her son responded to his male company and schools welcomed the input from male mentors.

The 'let us talk' approach appeared to work with the pupils both in and out of schools. The methods of this organisation in encouraging young persons to open up and discuss issues of concern to them both individually and in groups is considered helpful in that it recognises that the pupils would need to work out the part that they may play in achieving their academic potential and preventing exclusions. It also supports them in the 'problems they encounter' that Pablo highlights, such as 'the way that they're seen by their peers and then by the outside world'. Perry's assessment seems to be correct, that the young persons benefit both academically and through the development of interpersonal skills by discussing issues such as how they portray themselves versus how they would like to portray themselves, and subjects such as drugs and emotions.

Mediaid's open, businesslike, 'non-confrontational' and inclusive approach would seem to have an important role to play as it appeals to the young persons, their families, schools, LEAs and other agencies. Significantly, however, to become more successful in supporting parents' appeals over exclusions, Mediaid had to recourse to the less 'softly softly' stance of employing a trained barrister. For parents wishing to know 'where do we turn' when they are involved in the exclusions process, Advocaid would be such an organisation. It is to Advocaid that the next chapter now turns.

Chapter 6

Advocaid: 'We're here for the child'

A Black parents' advocacy organisation

Advocaid: Advocacy

Advocaid provides community-based support independent from the school in the form of advocacy to parents in their interaction with schools. Advocacy is defined as representation on behalf of a parent in respect of difficulties the parent may be having with schools. As the etymology implies, an advocate is intended to represent parents' interests and in cases of exclusions may, indeed, act in a stronger support role analogous to defending a client.

This independent voluntary organisation, the most established of the organisations, has been active since 1989. Education has from the onset formed the core of the work of the organisation. A firmly established reputation has been gained for supporting African and Caribbean families with children experiencing exclusion from schools. It was due to the increased number of requests for support by parents over educational matters that the Parent Empowerment Project was established as an extension of the long-standing work of the organisation. The main rationale of the Parent Empowerment Project was to 'represent children's interests' on a variety of educational matters and to empower parents to provide such representation themselves, particularly but not exclusively in matters of exclusion. The position of the organisation in relation to exclusions is described vividly in its literature: exclusions are 'Wasteful, Destructive, Discriminatory'. Advocaid has always therefore espoused a 'Nil Exclusion Policy'. The strong anti-racist perspective is embedded in the rationale. Documentation refers for example to supporting parents to 'challenge stereotyping within teaching attitudes and the curriculum' and 'nurturing cultural and racial identity'. Annette, an African Caribbean advocate, consistent with all members of staff and volunteers interviewed, stated in an interview that she believed it to be vital that 'Black parents are able to turn for support to an *independent* organisation like Advocaid'. A consultant's report produced for the organisation made the distinction clear:

Advocacy is different from mediation. Mediation attempts to hold the balance and build bridges between pupils and teachers and home and school, both of which are important in finding practical alternatives to exclusion. Advocates assist, support and represent children and parents in situations characterised by a gross imbalance of power, no matter the reassurance of adjudicating panels in the conduct of hearings and appeals.

Support to parents: four cases

To illustrate how this process operates, the cases of four specific sets of parents will now be reported. The first case discussed will be Josette, whose child was identified by the school as having special educational needs.

Josette: support required

> I was desperate because I didn't know anything about exclusion and all that sort of thing before, it was all very new to me.
> (Juliette: African Caribbean parent of Donovan)

I first met Josette when she visited the organisation with her son Donovan to have a meeting with an advocate to work through strategies for an exclusions meeting. She was an appropriate choice since I had met her personally as well as knowing from the files that her details would be relevant to the study. Josette enlisted the support of the organisation as her son was likely to be permanently excluded and she wanted an advocate to accompany her to the exclusions meeting. From the reports of Josette and the advocate, as well as written correspondence, a picture emerged of a child with special educational needs. The nature of the special needs may tentatively be implied from information supplied by his mother:

> He's quite a wilful child. Got a mind of his own. I give him more attention. He was always a demanding child, a very physical child, that gives problems at school. He's got lots of energy. The teacher can't cope with children like that.

She explained that he was not yet designated to have sufficient special educational needs to receive 'proper help'. In the meantime, she describes herself as 'at a loss ... He's fallen through the net. Obviously there's a problem but he's not getting the best help available'. From the advocate and parent, a picture emerged of the situation at school that eventually led to the decision to permanently exclude Donovan. His mother cited 'there's an agenda behind it. They've got to clean up the school. Like when the governors were coming in. They told me I've got to keep him at home for three days.' From the reports from the organisation and the mother, later verified by the home–school liaison teacher at the school, it had been under Special Measures after a negative Ofsted Inspection, what the mother referred to as 'Under some sort of special examination'. She had, she said, 'read the report, which had said they were not teaching the kids properly ... It talked about underachievement and punctuality'.

Josette did not appear to be completely blaming the school: 'It's easy to blame other people. He's got to take responsibility, look at *his* part' (her emphasis – indicated on transcript). She informed me that she had made an appointment to speak to the home–school liaison officer who had explained the procedures about the exclusions. She seemed to welcome his input, explaining that she knew him from before:

> When Donovan first started school he was doing parenting classes, I went to them. I thought it would be helpful. I went to the parenting classes just to show interest. In secondary school there's not much contact, not like primary school.

Josette discussed how she believed the transfer to secondary school had affected her son. 'He's always in trouble, now he sees himself as a bad child. He doesn't feel good. There's no focus on the positive. We keep getting letters home and I have to keep challenging him.'

'It's such a headache', reported Josette. Other reasons for her headache emerged during an interview. As a single parent, she had several other children apart from Donovan, and was combining this with part-time study. 'I'm doing counselling ... I haven't been able to do much work. It's kinda' heavy stuff, dealing with emotions.' Other factors were revealed, almost inadvertently. 'He was staying at my sisters 'cos we've got mice in the house. They're coming in through the central heating. We share a communal one.'

Josette: Advocaid support provision

Josette, like other parents interviewed, heard about the Parent Empowerment Project through *The Voice*, a leading national newspaper aimed at the African and Caribbean community:

> I was reading *The Voice* and I saw the article and I felt really relieved and I rang up straight away to get some advice and stuff ... and he was positive, he was really reassuring. When you're in a panic you can't think.

In supporting Josette, the organisation first assuaged her panic. This was made clear not just through Josette's own confirmation but more vividly through sitting in on her interview with an advocate, which enabled me to observe the process of support in action and to make notes, although I did not participate. Josette was visibly distressed at first while her son, Donovan, for the most part, sat quietly. The advocate reassured her that they would be able to help. Observation revealed that the majority of the time was spent on *listening* to Josette, after encouraging her to explain the situation so that they could be clear about all the factors leading up to the current situation, probing to find out more information. In response to Josette's expressed need for 'advice and stuff' the advocate provided information on how the exclusions process operated and on the options available, clarifying her questions along the way. He also went through with her some letters from the school that he had asked her to bring, underlining and explaining points. The interview lasted fifty minutes, during which I was able to see a change in Josette from her initial distress to seeming more reassured and positive, especially after the advocate agreed that he would accompany her to the school exclusion meeting. At this stage I asked whether she would allow me to conduct an interview during the following week, salient details of which are reported above. The result of the exclusions meeting was that the school made the decision to permanently exclude Donovan. On asking the school's reasons Josette replied,

> They said he wasn't learning anything and that he was stopping other people from learning. They said they'd tried everything. They'd put him on report but then he wouldn't get the reports filled in. They were saying that he'd seen a school counsellor and that had stopped it for a while.

From the perspective of the advocate who had accompanied her, the school 'didn't really listen' at the hearing. When asked whether she wanted to appeal against the exclusion, with the organisation's assistance, Josette's response was clear that she would not.

Michelle: support required

The case Michelle brought to the organisation concerned her 16-year-old son, Trevor. 'I think it all started really to get out of hand in secondary school. From he set foot in that door they knew he had landed.' He had, said Michelle, 'behavioural problems' in primary school but not like at secondary school where 'he did something every month till the day they kicked him out of school'. When probed about the type of things, the response was:

> To me, it was always nit picking things ... His *hat*, walking into school with his hat on his head. It wasn't allowed. But it just so happened. As he walked through the gate they said, Trevor, take your hat off ... I said Trevor, they've got binoculars, they're looking for you ... Then they'd

hang on to the hat. He'd go mad. He'd want his hat back. And yet, you'd find others. Well, they're not interested in all the others, *are* they ... ? I used to see the boys going into school walking through the gates with their hat on. It just got a bit petty sometimes.

Michelle, born in Britain of Jamaican parents, cited racism as a factor affecting her son's treatment. 'They'll always be racist ... It's hard, because they have to do so much. Because although it could be Trevor and a white boy for a job, same qualifications but they would find something and give the white boy at the end of the day.'

According to Michelle, despite the 'petty' incidents described above, she:

> always told them, don't tell me Trevor's behaviour gives you cause for concern, *call* me. I don't want to hear that this has happened and that has happened and then when you're gonna suspend him that's when I'm hearing everything, so I was in the school quite a lot. I went to *all* the meetings. I've got this; I've got to call it a dossier, on Trevor. And if he was supposed to have done all ... most of it ... I tell you he'd be up in court. The amount of things. If he sneezed. It looked like it was written down. So when there were meetings, it was always produced. It always had the latest date on it.

It was on being informed that she was to attend a meeting regarding Trevor's exclusion that she contacted Advocaid. On being asked whether she had any other type of support she mentioned her long-term partner, following her divorce from Trevor's father. 'I'm not saying he's not supportive, I can talk to him at the end of the day but he works all kinds of hours, my hours are better for going into school. We both work. We don't sort of sit around and wait for things to happen.' Accordingly, she took the initiative to contact Advocaid.

Michelle: Advocaid support provision

In response to her telephone request, Michelle was provided with the support of Annette, an African Caribbean advocate. 'I was *so* happy with her', was her response, describing Annette as 'a Black woman who understands'. She explained how helpful if was to have Annette preparing her for the meeting and agreeing to represent her. At the exclusions meetings, she and Annette were, she said, 'told all these new things, new excuses [such as] they weren't prepared for [Trevor] when he first started the school, as sometimes the kids come to the school before the records'. As Michelle explained,

> All this I heard at the exclusions meeting ... what they could have done, if they had his report, is say, right, we've got this child coming in; he's

got this behavioural problem. Keep an eye on him. Watch for anything out of the ordinary ...

and, as she explained above, *call* her. Instead, she was faced with the exclusions hearing where, as she described, 'this dossier went to all them at the top of the table, and then there was Annette and me on my side here and the school was on the other side'.

This view was consistent with that of Annette, discussing the case later, who referred to 'inconsistencies' in the school's documentation. These, she said, were 'grounds to appeal against the decision to exclude' especially bearing in mind some of the 'new' evidence. She explained that this all seemed very typical, from her experience working for the organisation and representing parents. 'It's important for parents not to just accept what the school says', she stated, and 'Advocaid would have supported her [Michelle] all the way.' On the other hand, she pointed out that 'I can understand how people don't want to go through all that ... after all that time, Michelle was just glad he's out of there.' Michelle's view was that she 'couldn't have asked for better support' [than Annette], 'she was great and really showed that she knew her stuff'. In the face of the 'dossier' however, she felt that it 'all totted up' and that the school was able to 'say they had helped ... It was like he'd had exclusions, then expulsions, and then "in house" exclusions – where he stays in this unit inside the school'. She referred to previous times, before contacting Advocaid: 'I used to have to go into school and collect the work 'cos he was not allowed back until I met with teachers to discuss the next move.' She was 'tired, fed up, and it was all sewn up, even with Annette, they'd still get him out and even if we won they'd make sure and get him as soon as he sets foot in the door again'. Michelle explained how, after the decision to exclude, Trevor was off school for nearly a year and was now in a Pupil Referral Unit. 'I hate the word but he's getting an education still'. She discussed how when he was at school, 'he never had any bad marks, I'm not bragging, he's very intelligent you know'.

As with Josette, I was able to glean indications of Michelle's socio-economic circumstances from the interview with Michelle and discussions with the advocate. Michelle explained that her job as a medical administrator was '*supposed* to be a good job ... I'm at a stage where I'm stuck in a job I don't want to be in'. Moreover, as she explained, she 'didn't want the same thing to happen to Trevor' (her son).

I don't even want Trevor in this country, because this country isn't going to give him anything. Take his education, take what he knows and take it elsewhere ... As far as I'm concerned the school's kicked him out ... If he can go to another country and learn a lot more and be appreciated more for what he knows all the better for him.

Aduah: support required

Aduah, a Nigerian mother of Ola, a primary school boy, heard of Advocaid through an advice centre not aimed specifically at the Black community. Like Michelle, I was able to interview her at home where she explained how her son started getting into trouble after a new head teacher arrived at her son's school and her son was now 'up for exclusion'. She explained the attitude of the school before she enlisted the support of Advocaid:

> They always think that all Black women, they can just do anything with them. Before I got Annette, their way and their manner ... I was just an unmarried African woman who doesn't know what I want in my life ... because they think that all Black people are just no hopers ... Nothing.

She seemed keen not to be classed in the same way as 'all Black women'. I asked if she became involved in activities at the school, to which she responded: 'I don't because I don't have the time. I have these children. I have my work, I have my course.' Being separated from her husband with four boys, she was now pursuing a university course part time, whilst working in what she called a 'low type of job, just to earn money while I'm doing my degree'. She related how 'they're always calling me on my mobile when I'm in the middle of a lecture'. She appeared keen to report that:

> His dad is a lawyer. My own family and his family. We are all educated. I did my A levels here. Only because I was working and having them, otherwise I would have finished my education.

Aduah was contemplating sending Ola, her son, 'back home'. 'Even if they say he is a trouble maker, he will get qualifications more than here.' Explaining why the school may have this view, she stated:

> They say look at him, he's *big* but it's not *his* fault he's big. All my children are big. That is how he *is*. He hasn't got any malice in him. But some people, the headmistress, says he hits hard. What can I do? That is how he behaves.

She also believed that he 'doesn't hit harder than some of the other boys'. She expanded on this theme:

> And also they say we're aggressive. It's not aggressive, that is how you *are*. Like me, if I'm talking you might think I'm *angry*. I'm not angry. Each individual has their own way of responding to things. I cannot expect you to behave like me because I'm *not you*. But they expect him to behave like other children. Even those from Africa and from over here. They are different ... I hope if I take him back home ... there you

are free ... Unlike here, the society has it that you must be soft, you must be gentle.

Racism was given as another reason for sending him back home. 'When he goes back home, there all of us are the same colour. There's nothing like racism.' It was also revealed during the course of the interview that the headmistress had wanted to start procedures for her son to have a Statement of Special Educational Needs (like Josette's son) because of the above type of behaviour.

Aduah: Advocaid support provision

In seeking support over the above situation, Aduah revealed how, before Advocaid, she had tried another organisation for Black parents (not one of those being studied here). 'All he wanted was to have him statemented. The man dealing with it, I didn't find him helpful at all. He came to the review meeting, he wanted him statemented.' Again, she contrasted this with Africa. 'There's nothing like statementing back home.'

When I asked about any other sources of support she referred to her husband. She informed me that although they were now separated, her son 'sees his dad every day, nothing lost'. She stated that 'the school doesn't understand this, they just see me as a single parent'. Partly, she said, that was because when she went to meetings at the school she 'didn't want him to go ... he would want to shout at the headmistress ... when he goes there he will bang on the table'. It was Annette, she said, who 'represented' her at an exclusions meeting with the head teacher and governors. The word 'represented' seemed in keeping with her view that Annette was like having her own lawyer:

> Annette, she's a lovely girl and she knows what she's doing. I said to her why don't you try and become a lawyer? You know the questions, the everything. Seriously, this girl. I wouldn't in my wildest dream have thought we could have got that far. If not for her ... say why don't you develop it because you are doing it. You would be good if you went to court. I tell you. The way she presents all these questions.

Annette explained in a later discussion that this was one of the cases where she had enough time to 'go through all the paperwork, line by line'. More usually, she explained, 'they tell the parent at the last minute [and] by the time we are able to get involved it's a crisis'. She worked with 'whatever situation I find myself with'. On relating Aduah's comments to Annette, she told me that at one time she had considered studying law but 'At the moment, I like what I'm doing to help the Black community.'

From Aduah's perspective, she had certainly been helped by Annette. 'She's quietly spoken but she gets her message across. She would take her turn but she would intimidate all these people ... Annette put fear into them. I tell you.' Her expressed faith in Annette was depicted as being irrespective of whether they won or lost. If they lost, she said, it would be only 'Because they have already made their decisions. They know that we have a case.'

Maureen: support required

Maureen enlisted support over her child, Pauline, who was in year 10 prior to the following situation, as described in her interview that led to her involvement with parent support organisations:

> I got a phone call from my daughter's school saying that they're sending her home with a letter because there was some incident at school. I asked the person what had gone wrong and she said it was all in the letter. Anyway, when my daughter came home the letter stated that there have been some incidents over the last few weeks and also there was a serious incident so therefore could I remove her from the school.

The main reasons for the exclusion, I was told, was that Pauline had 'been involved in a fight with another girl on a bus, where she had cut one of the girl's extension plaits'. Maureen was informed of this only when she attended a meeting at the school ... 'She said for the last two weeks there had been incidents ... she was late for school, she didn't do homework and she didn't go to school some of the time ... which I wasn't aware of'. Maureen seemed very concerned that this had all taken place without her knowledge and related how she had asked the teacher to take her child back into school and was told no. The teacher, according to Maureen:

> Gave the impression that my child didn't get on with any teachers. I said to her well can you prepare some work. She said she asked the teachers but nobody was prepared to do that. And I thought oh my God, don't tell me my child is that bad so no teacher is prepared to send her work. Anyway, I left, I was upset, I was crying and so on.

Maureen was visibly distressed at the memory but continued, 'No satisfaction. They wouldn't give her any work. They wouldn't take her back.' In attempting to establish the nature of the school's 'request' that her child leave, I asked, 'Is that on a permanent basis?' to which she responded in a somewhat uncertain manner, 'Well exclusion, I guess it's permanent.' On probing however, she stated categorically, 'No. She's not excluded. They're not saying that she's excluded. They've asked me to remove her. In other words, to take her out without them having to.' On being asked about where she turned for help she said, after waiting about two weeks (while her daughter was still at home) she 'decided to try other people and organisations, to see if [she] could get some help and one organisation said in fact she should be in school because she's not actually excluded'.

Having obtained this information she went to the school accompanied by a Black representative she had learned of through a Caribbean woman working for an LEA. According to Maureen, no one from the school would see her but someone spoke to the representative and 'when she came back she [the representative] wasn't happy. She said the teacher was extremely rude and wouldn't accept her child back into the school. She advised me that I should still take my child into school the next day so I did'. As she recounted, she did return the following day and:

> Asked for the principal. They said she wasn't there. I spoke to the deputy head who confirmed that the principal wasn't there and said that I should go home. She was trying to arrange some work for my daughter and she'd send it.

The deputy head telephoned her indicating that he would speak to the Chair of governors then contact her but in the meantime would send some work. Although the work did arrive, Maureen seemed especially concerned that her daughter should have taken two of her mock exams the week before. By that time her daughter entered the room and interjected, 'No, not two, all of them. All of my mock exams are coming up.' She explained that she wanted to pass her exams and 'go on to study law'. She said she had written a letter of apology and that the parent of the girl whom she had cut the extension plait had also written.

Maureen: Advocaid support provision

From her interview, correspondence she showed me and interviews with the advocate who was handling her case, it seemed that Maureen had approached a number of sources for advice. However, apart from Advocaid, other organisations, one of which turned out to be Mediaid, were, she said, 'useless'. When asked why she believed this was the case, she said that 'The person at Mediaid had a right go at Pauline. She was already being punished. I didn't like his approach. He wrote a letter *begging* the headmistress to take Pauline back.' She said she believed that he 'was on the side of the headmistress'.

In contrast, at Advocaid, she said 'they were so good'. The case was discussed with the advocate who explained that her daughter was excluded permanently. In Maureen's opinion, at the exclusions hearing 'they presented a really good case'. The only reason they lost, she believed, was that 'they'd already made up their mind'. This belief was echoed in a separate interview with Maureen, who spoke of a Black teacher at the school who:

was saying that they only go so far and when there's an exclusion or when they want to exclude a child it's like they don't seem to take note of what they're saying. They just sort of make up their minds and it doesn't matter what that Black teacher, or anybody else is saying, they just don't want to know.

Maureen reported that she believed the school was racist in its handling of her daughter's case but said, 'I just can't deal with them right now because I just need to get her into school.' Her first choice was one which was 'good' in terms of its examination results. 'When I asked them [the school] about when she got excluded they said it's going to be very hard for Pauline to get into there.' It was indeed and she was turned down. Her next attempt was a Roman Catholic school. She reported that on attending the interview she was informed that the school had believed they were Roman Catholics and asked for a letter from the local church. As she explained, however, 'Pauline hasn't been there for about two years.' Maureen contrasted her experience with the girl who had been excluded with Pauline over the same incident. 'What really annoys me is that they have got Elizabeth in a very good school.' Her explanation was that 'Obviously, Elizabeth's mother is white and Elizabeth is mixed race ... so that's where there's the difference'. She also related that when she wasn't able to get her child in a school, she refused the local Pupil Referral Unit and her daughter was now having home tuition.

Other aspects of Advocaid's work in supporting parents

Exclusions advocacy training

In accordance with their rationale of empowerment, exclusions advocacy training was an integral element of the support on offer to parents and other community members. A publicity leaflet for the training describes the aims as: 'To equip participants with the knowledge and skills necessary to act as pupils'/parents' advocates in exclusions hearings and appeals.' The participants being aimed at were parents and others from the African and Caribbean community, with the organisation's volunteers being encouraged to attend. Having undertaken a review of their training sessions as part of my 'volunteer' work with the project, the research undertaken and the evaluation report produced provide information about the nature of such training and how it was intended to support Black parents in supporting their children's education. The training aimed to help the participants to arm themselves with the legal and procedural matters of the exclusions process by exploring how they would deal with case studies based on real-life experiences faced by families the organisation had supported. The case study report was entitled 'Safeguarding our Children'. The mainly African and Caribbean participants were provided with a comprehensive training package of wide-ranging and up-to-date information showing the legal aspects of exclusion procedures and findings from research about exclusions, especially in relation to the Black community. In discussions with the facilitator after the event, he stated that this was 'helpful in putting the case studies in a wider context'.

In the informal verbal feedback from the training, the participants expressed the view that they particularly liked 'working with real cases'. This was observed in the purposeful way the groups participated in their different cases. These included, for example, letters from schools to parents and their replies (names protected for anonymity). Even the researcher was surprised at the vast amount of paperwork each case produced and discussions with the training facilitator revealed that he considered it important that the participants were aware of the scope of paperwork that could arise from each case. He did, however, 'talk through' the paperwork with them prior to the group working on a role-play exercise of sifting through the documents for evidence and potential extenuating circumstances.

The verbal feedback from the participants on the sessions audio taped and observed was positive. 'I'm very pleased ... I feel there's a powerhouse in here. I just want to say congratulations to the group and continue with the good work.' The participants covered a range of age, community interests, socio-economic status, gender, and educational and work background. As one participant enthused, 'It seems really good that you're getting more and more people ... people in the community, parents and everybody ... involved in the advocacy project.' The 'powerhouse' of people that Advocaid attracted to its training included a significant minority who did not live in a culturally diverse community: 'Absolutely excellent. I've really enjoyed it. I come from [–shire] and you see one Black face in a year if you're lucky, I've really enjoyed it ... it's been a very positive experience.' All expressed their commitment to use the knowledge gained for the benefit of others in their community. A Black male participant for example, declared,

> What I'm really pleased about is the number of groups like yourself who're out there. People don't know ... there are so many people who say ... we're not going to accept what the schools tell us ... they are finding avenues of protest ... questioning what the schools tell them.

Putting advocacy training into action

As part of the process of validating these findings, telephone interviews were conducted to ascertain whether any of the participants had realised their intention of using their training. Available feedback suggested that the training was being used both directly and indirectly. Sandra is an example of one who applied her training in a number of different ways. It is also a critical case in illustrating several features that applied to many of the parents interviewed during the fieldwork. Some time after the training Sandra was involved in supporting her brother, who had been temporarily excluded. One of the factors related is that the head teacher told her informally that it was in her brother's 'best interests' not to return to school after he had been temporarily excluded twice. In this instance, however, using information from the training, its advocate facilitator and other agencies, Sandra was able to challenge the school's decision as described below.

> We made the school realise that this is unacceptable and we're not accepting this for these reasons and that at this moment with Damian's future being a young Black boy I don't feel the school is doing anything to help him [...] the school has failed him because issues they brought up were going back years and we had no knowledge of most of what had been logged about him and he didn't agree with some of the things that they'd recorded on him.
>
> (Sandra, advocacy training participant and sister of excluded boy)

Sandra expressed the view that her eventual success in challenging the school was partly 'based on the fact that I had a fair amount of knowledge and I knew people who had a certain amount of power like Julian', an advocate from the organisation. Upon my saying, 'from what you've said, you don't sound as if you need representing', she emphatically responded that she did. The result of their combined intervention was that the governors decided not to exclude Sandra's brother. The reason Sandra provided was that this was 'because they knew they had to have *very* good grounds as to permanent exclusion. They've turned everything around and they're trying to support Damian [her brother] in the best way possible'. The support included him being provided with a mentor and having an IEP, this being an 'Individual Education (Action) Plan of targets agreed by the school and family, based on the child's needs. Other, more peripheral, use of the training was cited, for example a participant using recordings from the training for a radio programme, as part of his studies, and a newly qualified teacher who used the information in her work.

Parental support provision: Education Conference Workshops

'The Parenting Role in Supporting Children and Representing their Interests at School' has been selected to report as an example of the workshops and conference presentations of Advocaid. The aim of the conference of which the workshop played a part was to 'highlight the opinions and experience of parents and pupils who are at the sharp end of the system' (conference report). The rationale behind the parents' workshop was articulated as follows:

> It was agreed that there was a need to reject the pathological view of various agencies when discussing the education/training of Black parents. Instead, the workshop proposed to draw on the positive qualities, whereby parents recognised the nature of problems experienced by their children and were determined to support them in gaining justice and the best possible opportunities to develop their potential.
>
> (Conference report: p. 30)

The workshop report highlights one of the major pieces of advice on offer to the parents. The facilitator explained, for example, that it is:

> important not to just drop one's child at the school gates. Colour doesn't change upon entering the schooling institution. Children experience the same kind of oppression and racist practices as adults in the wider community. Parents must become actively involved as governors and members of the Parent Teacher Association.

Observations from participating at the conference reveal the parents being provided with ample opportunity to air and share their views, concerns and problems, guided by a facilitator, being encouraged to suggest courses of action before consolidating the main points for presentation to the wider conference. This workshop was one of the most well attended, and provided opportunity for analysis. If there was one dominant theme, it was that expressed cogently by a participant, in the Jamaican proverb, 'Fowl can't ask hawk to protect chicken', which produced a spontaneous round of applause. If the 'chickens' were their children and the parents the fowl, then in the perspective of that particular parent and the facilitator and other parents partaking in the applause, the hawk would be the majority of the school teaching staff. The type of protective strategies which it was suggested that parents could undertake included, for example, to actively listen and communicate with their children on a regular basis about their school experience, to discuss any intended course of action with them before proceeding and to generally be seen to be supportive and trusting of them. Although the facilitator agreed that children were not always particularly communicative it was emphasised that such communication was vital. Other 'protective' strategies for the families suggested by the facilitator are included in the workshop report:

> If in doubt or if feeling any trepidation, parents should ensure that they found someone to go with them to such meetings. It was important to

make notes of the meetings and to report back to one's child as soon as possible. If inaccurate assertions were made, it was important to correct them with an early telephone call or letter.

(Workshop conference report: p. 31)

During the discussion, parents mentioned 'doubts' and 'trepidation' in relation to their contact with schools. Others were more angry and used words such as 'rude', 'discrimination' and 'racism' about their experiences, and those of their children, with some teachers and schools. The workshops and training provided observable evidence of how the rationale of the organisation, as exemplified in policy documentation, was reflected in practice and how this was received by the parents present.

The above illustrations were helpful in adding to the understanding of the work of the organisation gained from the parents' case studies. In considering the way that Advocaid assisted the parents enlisting their support, not just those revealed in the case study or the above, several themes emerge. These themes form key issues to be considered in developing understanding of the work of Advocaid in supporting the parents, and the factors that appeared to facilitate or constrain its impact. In the following sections, the key themes emerging from this broader range of data will be presented.

Key themes and issues

Exclusions

Exclusions were the key theme as they were the dominant reason for parents enlisting the support of the organisation and formed the bulk of its work, as revealed in its files and record of work. All the cases of parents coming into the office whilst I was present were associated with either temporary or permanent exclusion. This was, of course, unsurprising given its key aim of supporting parents over exclusions. Interrogation of data, including aspects such as the occupation of the family and marital status, did not produce a profile of a 'typical' or likely parent whose child would be excluded. Attendance or otherwise at functions such as parents' evenings did not appear to offer a preventative measure. The question about their relationship with the school tended to elicit the information that they went to parents' evenings, even if they were unable to attend other events:

I went to all the parents' evenings and also because of the type of work I do. I do residential social work and it's really hard for me to get time off because I do sleep-overs so it's really hard but I've attended all the parents' evenings.

(Caribbean mother of year 10 GCSE student)

Similar to the parents' position, cross-case comparison of interview data revealed that of the cases reported, previous to the fixed-term exclusion, the girls in particular were described by their parents as being considered to be a 'good' or at least not a 'bad' student in terms of them not hearing from the school about problems regarding behaviour or work. Maureen, for example, said of Pauline,

> The reason why I think it is so unfair is because she's never ever been in trouble before. Academically, she is doing really well, she takes part in so many things in the school, she does talent contests and things like that, she has won two years in a row. She is a really good singer, she is on the front cover of their prospectus. I've never had a bad report about her, never. All her reports have been very good.

I was proudly shown the prospectus.

In the cases studied, not just those reported, evidence from Advocaid's files revealed that once children were permanently excluded from a school, it was difficult for the parents to enrol them in another and the children were more likely to be allocated to a Pupil Referral Unit. Participant observation at the office revealed that Advocaid tended to concentrate on their advocacy work as this was the most pressing concern.

'I was desperate'

Parents, as interview evidence previously reported, tended to telephone Advocaid in 'panic' and 'desperation'. 'I was desperate for my child to be helped' was one such comment. Examination of correspondence from the schools attended by these parents revealed a relatively brief period before notice of impending meetings. By the time the parents, like Michelle and Aduah, had tried other places, Advocaid had little time to prepare its case. Their intervention was thus needed at a point of crisis, usually in the form of representing the family at a meeting.

It emerged from comparing the different demographic profiles that this sense of desperation was not confined to parents in socio-economic circumstances like that of Josette. Carmen, a parent not from the cases reported, was a senior manager in a public sector organisation, living in very comfortable surroundings, as revealed when Julian and I met her at home and then accompanied her to that which she termed a 'grant maintained' school, over the temporary exclusion of her son. Her 'desperation' was, she said, because the school was 'abusing their power'. She explained that her child had a 'good record' and 'received an award for good conduct' the previous year. She was 'not happy', she said, and felt that 'if he were white they wouldn't have wanted to exclude him ... the other child, a girl, didn't get excluded'.

Power imbalance

The documentation of Advocaid points to 'power imbalance' as a primary factor that enables such decisions. A report by a management consultant on the work of Advocaid states explicitly:

> The power imbalance within schools can be summarised as the power and support given to schools versus the absence of information, support and access to assistance provided to enable parents to effectively represent the interests of the child. Advocates and parents repeatedly complain of the acceptance by appeal bodies of evidence that would not be accepted in other judicial or quasi-judicial hearing.

In analysing the frequency of examples where 'power' related words were used, one of the most striking is the parents' workshop at the conference where Suzette, a participant, gave the following advice: 'Know your importance as a parent. You have the power, nobody else has the power. You have the power as a parent to actually make a difference in your child's education.'

Sandra, whom it may be recalled was the woman who had supported her brother after attending the training, echoed this theme. She pointed out in the follow-up interview that since the training she had set up a lone parents' support group where, she states:

> I've given guidelines based on some of what I remembered which I must say isn't a lot and my recent experience with my brother in supporting him so that was brought back to the group and shared and giving the parents that sort of empowerment that yeah, although teachers are professionals they don't have the ultimate control of what happens to your children.

The way that she has managed to put some of the training into action despite, as she says, not remembering 'a lot' has provided understanding of some of the ways in which the organisation has managed to provide a range of persons with the skills of advocacy to work within their community. This type of empowerment, of a more proactive stance, could be contrasted with that observed in the numerous 'crisis' type situations of impending exclusions meetings, where, as their documents revealed and parents such as Edward portrayed, there was an imbalance of power. Edward's case also provides insights into the nature of the 'power' of the organisation for parents who might otherwise be 'in isolation'.

> As a parent in isolation the school is likely to tell you that it is just your child. They're shaming you. The teacher is isolating you. It's the age-old

process of divide and conquer. You're not aware that lots of Black children are going through this. You don't know all the stats. Advocaid has all the stats.

(Edward: West African parent)

Organisational culture

Several issues emerged about the organisation. First, there appeared to be organisational consistency in that all members of staff interviewed agreed on the importance of its strong anti-racist stance, with the support of the family being paramount. A practical organisational feature mentioned by many was the need for more time and staff. As an evaluation report noted, 'Advocaid seems to have become a victim of its own success', with an ever increasing workload. Field notes report that 'the different strands of its work seem to be competing for resources of time and staff'. In discussing this aspect, one of the Advocaid personnel informed me that through contact with a local government volunteering scheme they were able to use a regular supply of volunteers and that most of the permanent staff, including Annette, started off as volunteers. I was able to interview Lorrayne, one of the volunteers, in depth, who explained that after working with Advocaid, she felt that she had gained the confidence to put herself forward as a school governor and how 'shocked' she was when she received the letter of acceptance.

The volunteers, from my observations, made a significant contribution to the work of the organisation, undertaking many of its routine day-to-day operations. Technically, Julian was also a volunteer, even though, to all intents and purposes, he seemed to be at the helm of the organisation. Evidence from documents and other personnel revealed that he had performed all the funding applications and he seemed heavily involved in all aspects of the organisation's work. Julian and Annette both mentioned the need for more resources and Julian in particular stated that he spent a lot of time writing funding applications. It was explained that the keeping of detailed accurate records and reports about their work was important evidence to support such applications but was time consuming. The maintaining of a variety of statistics, from the detailed records of the nature of all telephone calls and the number and type of schools cited in the cases, was one of the features observed as part of the culture of this particular organisation. Julian had explained its importance in relation to providing evidence for funding applications and in seeing the 'wider picture'. Julian was, as explained, of white British heritage, with the rest of the staff of African and Caribbean heritage. Early field notes of observations at the LEA hearing suggest that the combination of a Black Caribbean woman and a white British man representing the parents appeared to be an effective strategy. Increasingly, tensions became more apparent in the internal dynamics, some of which were explicitly stated as race related. One worker stated, 'if you're desperate for your child to be helped it doesn't matter what colour the person is'. In contrast, in discussion with participants after a conference, a well-known Black community activist questioned Julian's credentials in fronting the organisation, suggesting that 'we have already as a community shown that we can organise ourselves'.

'Learn what you can learn. Get what you can get.'

'As a community', or at least as the members of the community who attended Advocaid training sessions and its conference where I observed and participated, and whose cases were brought to the organisation, the importance of educational qualifications for their children was a dominant and recurring theme. Pauline's mother, for example, explained that her child 'would like to pass her exams and go on to university and study law'. Pauline reiterated this aspiration. Michelle's advice for her son was, 'Don't sit on your arse like I did, learn what you can learn, get what you can get.' Aduah had said of her son, 'He is quite intelligent and he will work. I would like him to get as much education as he wants, qualifications and the discipline.' For these, as explained in the portrait of the family, she was sending him back to Africa.

The school effect

Data from the organisation's records and files and discussions with its personnel revealed that some schools in the local area were disproportionately represented in the cases being brought to them. Julian's assertion was that the schools that had failed Ofsted were more likely to exclude. This belief, he explained, was based on Advocaid's records of cases across the years. One recalls Josette's explanation of being asked to keep her child at home during Ofsted. A report from Advocaid points to 'pressure on schools to exclude due to league tables'. Edward's view of the way that 'zero tolerance' was used in some schools and his contrast between different schools' interpretation of this was explained as affecting the children: 'Children know if you're for or against them, even at that young age. If it's all negative kids get a feeling of entrenchment. They're fighting against the system.'

The 'school effect' emerged as a feature of schools per se. Classroom management was a feature highlighted as a general issue for schools in the advocacy training sessions. The facilitator pointed to the need for training in classroom management, cultural issues and interacting with parents from different cultures to be aimed at teachers in general and inexperienced teachers in particular. Examples about schools in general were also provided by a conference facilitator. He discussed 'the value of schools being accountable to pupils and parents' and made the plea, to loud applause, that:

We need to find a way that assertiveness, intelligence and a keen sense of justice are seen and valued as qualities to be developed and not as arrogance and insubordination to be punished.

He ended with discussing 'a fundamental lack of trust and mutual respect between teachers in schools and the pupils and parents'.

Institutionalised racism

Both facilitators and participants at the conference cited racism as a major concern. Julian's definition of racism was

the view held by white people of themselves as superior and Black people as inferior, a view suppurating into individual and institutional attitudes and practices and proving an obstacle therefore to bringing about any lasting and fundamental change in British society unless vigorously combated at every level.

Various occurrences of when racism was mentioned during the workshop and conference were recorded in field notes. One explicit mention by a participant, which implicitly referred to institutional racism, was to:

hold the racial element of it. That's institutional in everything we do. It doesn't matter if you're going into a shop to buy a packet of sweets or whether your child's in university. We're talking about institutionalised racism. That's a long term thing and we will continue to fight that every day. But what we can do as parents is to take an *active* stance. Make sure we attend not just parents' evenings but if there's an issue ... don't take things as gospel, go in and find out, try to resolve it [italics added].

Edward makes explicit reference to the racism of the head teacher at the school his child had been at previously:

Without a shadow of doubt that head teacher was racist. I remember asking why someone who didn't like the boys ever bothered to become a teacher. She said, 'I've been teaching Black kids in the inner cities for how many years'. I hadn't even *mentioned* the colour. She implied that Black kids were problems. I told her she was a racist. She said, as all racists do, ... 'some of my best friends are coloured'.

A culturally mixed school

On being asked to 'tell me about the cultural mix of the school' Edward replied:

It's very mixed but the school wasn't good at dealing with a culturally mixed school. I feel that they resented the fact that that they were dealing with inner city kids, with predominantly Black kids.

Carmen, the parent visited in the 'leafy suburb', explained that her son was one of 'only a handful' of Black children at the school and that she felt that 'they didn't want him there in the first place'.

In contrast, the process of cross-case comparison of answers to questions about the cultural mix of the school and the school's response reveals Lorrayne, the volunteer, as saying about her daughter's school:

I think they do quite a bit of work. They put aside special rooms for everyone that likes to pray. I found that quite interesting. It boosts the morale of the children. It helps. You're respected in what you do and your way of life.

With African Caribbean culture, I think they're getting somewhere. I walked into a music lesson the other day, they were playing different kinds of music. When I was at school it was all classical music. So they took a bit of their culture into that lesson, which was good, and they do that with cooking. My concern is that some teachers don't want to do anything like that.

Involvement with the child's school

Apart from the type of situation described in the case studies, the most frequently occurring type of involvement mentioned by the parents was attending parents' evenings. Carmen for example states, 'I go to all the meetings about my son's work but not to any of the social events, they don't appeal to me.' Lorrayne, however, was a school governor, who in her interview indicated that her 'drive to be there' was largely due to volunteering with Advocaid. Even she, however, said, 'most of the Black parents don't go to the social events put on by the school'.

Perceptions of Black mothers

Maureen, Pauline's mother, in her interview described how the school kept writing to her as Miss Jones. She explained that Pauline 'was always having to tell the school that I'm married'. Pauline corroborated this by explaining, 'They assume most Black people don't have fathers.' Aduah, as recalled, reported how she believed that the school perceived single Black women negatively and this was repeated by some of the participants at the workshop and conference sessions.

Gender issues: children

Data from Advocaid's workbook and files revealed the organisation being called upon to support more Black boys than girls. In her discussion with the school, on behalf of her mother, Sandra refers to the effects of Damian being a 'young Black boy'. Like Michelle, Trevor's mother, and most of the parents in the sample, they were in the position of supporting young Black boys in their interaction with schools, whether at secondary age as in this instance, or in the case of Edward whose sons were primary school students. There were of course examples, like Pauline, whose parents were supporting them over exclusions. Pauline's mother, Maureen, noted moreover that at the local PRU where she refused to send her daughter:

> It's full of Black boys and they're not doing anything, they've been excluded and they're not doing anything with these boys and I'm sorry, I'm not sending Pauline there. I told them that I refuse so she has home tuition, they pay for that.

The experiences of Lorrayne, a volunteer at Advocaid, provided further insights which may assist in developing our understanding from a parents' perspective:

> I find having had two girls and a boy I find it's very hard work with the boy. They're easily bored. It's harder for them to settle. So maybe in school ... especially with a hundred others ... their ego. I think this is half the problem. They wanna look big and look cool and everything and maybe little scuffles will break out. Whereas I found with the girls. You can sit down and say today we're gonna do this and then we're gonna do that.

Lorrayne's son, Tony, had been temporarily excluded and she approached Advocaid for initial support, following which she became a volunteer. Tony was attending an all-boys school, her first choice, for the following reasons:

> He comes from a family of predominantly female and I felt that because I am female and I am a single parent and I am a mother I didn't feel it was good for him to be constantly with women and girls all the time. As a boy growing up I felt he needed to be in a male environment. You know, dealing with the structure and the bonding.

Her interview reveals her noting the influence of Tony being in an all-boys school from year 7. 'The whole year 7. Boys together they mess about. Their ego takes over and they start cussing and everything. It starts off as a play thing and they get into a serious fight.' It was after a 'serious fight' that her son was excluded. At the time of writing neither of her girls, who were attending an all-girls school, had been excluded. She had selected the school on the basis that: 'When I was at school I felt I couldn't compete with the boys … Science … I wanted my girls to be in an environment where they could build up their confidence.'

> I think the school does a lot to encourage girls of all cultures to come forward … to speak about themselves. It's not just we do this and you learn this. I think it's very good … 'the best school for women of the future' is their slogan.

Choice

Other key issues surrounding the selection of schools emerged within the study. Claudette, another parent (not the subject of a case study), cited a scenario that was depicted fairly frequently within the data:

> She went there as a last resort, I didn't get my first choice. At the time I didn't want her to go to … girls. It has a lot of Black girls and the Ofsted report did not have a lot of positive things to say, it was very worrying. I applied to four schools in fact. The thing with this borough is that it's just the one choice you've got, which is pathetic really. There was another one we applied for in another borough but we didn't get in, so it was a last minute sort of panic. This one, I didn't have an awful lot of background but I thought it was an OK school … it was a middle class area, they would be getting good examination results and things like that. Ideally the kind of school I'd have liked her to go to was a kind of middlish school.

When probed, she explained that this would be one where there was more of 'a mixture'. Given her comment about the number of Black girls, my field notes record it interesting to note that, following the failure of an exclusions appeal where she was supported by Advocaid, Claudette's child was now at a school with almost 100 per cent Black children, run by Black staff. Pauline's mother had decided that she would also send her son to the same school and he had ended up obtaining five GCSE 'good' passes, which she felt he would not have received at his previous school where 'there were problems with the teachers'. Claudette's response to the school was:

> I prefer the teachers here. They're kind and they understand. The teachers at the other school, they didn't understand. They didn't listen to you. The teachers here, I don't know if it's because they're Black or what.

Carmen revealed that she chose her son's school because of good exam results. However, the adjective 'arrogant' was used to describe the teachers, suggesting that this was partly because the grant-maintained school was one where people were 'desperate' for their children to get into, 'so they can pick and choose'.

More Black teachers

Carmen was one of the parents from whom the role of Black teachers emerged in an unanticipated manner. Here, she explained 'they have one Black teacher there who tried to start a Black History club. Whilst Carmen 'thought it was a very good idea' she expressed concern that she 'wasn't sure how the school [would] react'. Maureen, Pauline's mother, had described the Black teacher at her daughter Pauline's school as supportive; but had felt that she was 'not listened to' by the school. She expressed the view that schools should 'have more Black teachers who understand Black kids'. On interviewing Maureen at her home I had the opportunity to meet the teacher who was providing Pauline with some home tuition. She was a Caribbean woman who fitted Maureen's description and explained that she thought that Pauline was 'very bright'.

Special educational needs

Another unanticipated emergent theme was that the instances of exclusions were found to include a number of pupils who were referred to, in the correspondence, as having special educational needs (SEN). For all but one of these, their needs were designated as 'behavioural' and all apart from Claudette's daughter were boys. The two persons who conducted most of the advocacy mentioned, in separate interviews, that parents they came into contact with did not seem to understand the procedures for pupils designated as having SEN. Among the parents interviewed, only Josette appeared to welcome the procedure, due to the potential for her son obtaining support, although she said that she 'didn't really understand all of it'. Others, like Aduah, were reluctant to accept the school designating their child as SEN. In the training session for advocates, the facilitator explained that SEN was a feature that many of the parents said they did not understand. One of the volunteers said that this would be an area for providing specific courses or information to parents, but 'again, lack of time ... we have to prioritise'.

The impact of Advocaid's support

Even with the help of volunteers, what was described by one of the advocates as 'the sheer volume' of their work on exclusions dominated their priorities. It was for this reason that Julian said he wanted the advocacy training to 'cascade within the community'.

The data did not identify even one incident where a parent expressed displeasure at the way Advocaid handled their case. The parent who eventually sent her child to a Black-run school explained how, before being supported by Advocaid, she was 'totally stressed out, I'm a single parent, I haven't got my family, my large family here. My parents are back home' (in Jamaica). In Edward's view, 'when you're on your own, you're an easy target, you can be easily manipulated; the school was not expecting the fight we gave them ... You become more willing to fight back through contact with Advocaid.' Aduah, as recalled, was effusive in her praise of Annette, her advocate, as was Michelle. Maureen, Pauline's mother, like Aduah, had experience of attempting to enlist the support of other organisations, both 'mainstream' and specifically aimed at Black parents, and both their interview data demonstrated that it was Advocaid they found most helpful. Edward, likewise, explains, 'we need groups like Advocaid who know that there's some fundamental questions that have to be addressed'. Knowing the right questions to ask, as well as being prepared to ask them, was what appeared to be being referred to here. One of the features of Advocaid that seemed to facilitate its credibility with the parents was that they considered that the group 'understood' Black families. Observational evidence at meetings, home visits, conference and workshops, suggested that Advocaid knew the culture of its client group and used this knowledge in all aspects of their work, a practical example being that participants for the advocacy training are able to select to attend on either the Saturday or Sunday to prevent clashes with Saturday schools or Seventh Day Adventist activity on a Saturday or other religious worship on a Sunday. A closer examination of the evidence increasingly suggested however that it was more than just knowledge or indeed understanding of culture and race issues that the parents appreciated; it was an unambiguous commitment to challenge unfair practices within an explicit anti-racist framework.

When parents were asked how their child's school reacted to having Advocaid involved, answers included: 'She was very upset ... She made us out to be Black militants', as expressed by Edward. Aduah, we noted before, expressed the view that it was because of the input of Annette, her advocate, that the school had enlisted the services of a lawyer.

Perhaps the last word about the organisation should be left to Annette, the advocate whose praises were sung by all who related being supported by her:

> By the time some parents contact Advocaid they have been passed from pillar to post. Some have given up hope of finding justice. Not all appeals are successful but all parents glory in the mere fact that their grievances were heard by those responsible for their suffering and the suffering of their child.

> (Annette, advocate)

Implications for schools

What, if anything, can schools learn from situations that have deteriorated to the crisis point of involvement in the school exclusion process? Instinctive and to some extent understandable reactions from some schools would emphasise that students who behave appropriately and do not breach school rules are not putting themselves in a situation of potential exclusion; that the learning of the majority of students should not be prevented by the negative behaviour of a few and that it is the responsibility of parents to support the school in its aims.

The case studies, however, lead to a less clear-cut picture. Some children with previously 'good' records were permanently excluded and it emerges quite strongly that sanctions were unevenly applied both across and within the schools portrayed. Behaviour such as fights between pupils that may lead to permanent exclusions in some of the schools may result in less severe actions by others. Within a school, parents noticed instances of inequitable application of school rules. At the most basic level, if, as in Michelle's case, a parent is able to point to evidence that some other boys attend school with their hat on whereas her son is reprimanded, it is difficult for a school to convince that parent that the school is not being 'petty' or discriminatory in singling out her child.

Policies and codes of conduct in relation to behaviour and to exclusions are likely to be part of a school's general documentation. These parents however, at the stage of being involved in the school exclusion process, did not consider that they even had the opportunity of going through the 'right' channels. The very channels themselves, as created by the schools, were believed by the parents and by Advocaid to be engineered to lead to the outcome desired by the school – i.e. permanent exclusions. From situations such as being presented with a 'dossier' of previous 'misconduct' at the exclusion panel, to parents being advised to remove their child from the school to prevent the school from taking that step, to microscopic scrutiny and recording of 'petty' incidents, the process was considered a 'put up job'. If, as the parents and Advocaid believe, some schools have 'already made their decision' before the appeals hearing, and governors are not seen to be impartial, it is unsurprising that these parents seek recourse to organisations such as Advocaid who 'know what questions to ask' and support them in appeals against decisions so that, at the very least, schools are obliged to listen and to provide answers.

If opportunities were provided regularly for the families to air their 'grievances' and the answers and actions of the school demonstrate that they had listened to the parents, this may, over time, lead to a more constructive dialogue with an enhanced understanding from both sides that the pupils are there to 'learn what they can learn and get what they can get' and that parents can contribute to this.

Like the pupils, some of the qualities displayed by the parents could usefully be engaged by the schools in roles such as school governorship, and their input and suggestions may enhance the quality, transparency and equality of some of the school's policies and practices which may act in preventing exclusions. Current barriers to such dialogue which would need to be overcome, however, including perhaps a cultural expectation that parents, like children, are 'expected to be soft, expected to be gentle'. Within agreed parameters, a school would need to be prepared for parents who would not see their role as merely 'rubber-stamping' decisions.

Some schools, e.g. that described by Carmen, provide social events to which parents are invited. This more relaxed setting is conducive to the fostering of more effective communication between home and school. Carmen, like other parents in the study, attends all the meetings about her child's work. She does not find the social events particularly appealing, however. 'Equality monitoring' of attendance at all school functions, including the more social of these, would reveal activities that appear to attract parents or particular groups of parents as well as alerting the school to any gaps in attendance. Where Black staff have shown interest in, for example, forming a Black History club, like the teacher in Carmen's son's school, this is to be encouraged and the teacher may have a role in enlisting the support of like-minded parents.

Some of the reasons that parents offer for thinking highly of the service provided by Advocaid offer key points of learning to schools. Advocaid both understood the needs of the families and allied this to practical measures which took their needs into account and demonstrated respect. Moreover, the parents welcomed an organisation with explicit commitment to challenge discriminatory practice, including the different manifestations of racism and cultural stereotyping.

Through the case studies, we learn of ways in which schools can demonstrate to parents, like Lorrayne, that 'you're respected in what you do and your way of life'. Unlike those head teachers who showed that they 'weren't used to dealing with a culturally mixed school', the curriculum and ethos of the school appeared welcoming to different cultural groups. What did not work for the parents was communicating with them in clichés such as 'some of my best friends are Black' or suggesting that because a head or other teacher has 'been teaching kids in the city for how many years' that made them an 'expert' in race issues or devoid of attitudes where a parent can state 'without a show of doubt that teacher is racist'.

In communicating with parents, 'little' actions, such as taking the trouble to address the parents by their correct title, and trying to include some positive letters and phone calls among any negative messages home, convey signals to which the families are likely to be more receptive. This would need to be joined to the 'bigger' actions, such as regular 'equality auditing' of policies including the collection of qualitative information from parents and pupils etc., to complement statistical returns to ascertain any differential impact on behavioural policies and exclusions for particular groups, including SEN pupils. The results from 'early warning' signals, communicated to parents in a timely and appropriate manner, is likely to reduce both the proportion of exclusions and the 'suffering' caused, not least to lost academic opportunities.

Implications for the advocacy support organisation

Given the stated perspective that, within their particular context, 'fowl can't ask hawk to protect chicken', factors that seemed to contribute to the parents' experience of feeling so supported by Advocaid was that the organisation 'believed in them' and, as several parents explained, 'was positive'. In turn, the parents trusted that Advocaid would protect their interests.

Advocaid clearly acts as a counterbalance to that which their management report describes as a 'woeful lack of advice, information and support for parents or carers seeking to represent the interest of pupils excluded or at risk of exclusion'. Their proactive stance in cascading information and providing in-depth training on exclusions and other schools-related matters was key to the empowerment they afforded. It allowed a wide range of community members to network and gain the knowledge, opportunity and confidence to challenge practices perceived to be unjust. A consequence of its positive impact on the parents was the type of wariness observed by members of the appeals panel. Sandra had reported copying in Advocaid in her correspondence with the school and she believed that the school knowing she had its support made the school 'more careful'. Her assertion that 'I think they'd have preferred if I didn't have all these strong Black people behind me' is indicative of a position where schools are unaccustomed to challenges of this nature. They enacted the policy statement that 'Black parents must organise to protect their children. Divisions and inequalities must be challenged' (parents' workshop report).

This was compared in one of their reports to LEA officials, who were 'sometimes placed in a position of inaction because of the delicate relationship between schools and the authority'. In the following chapter, we are shown how a group of parents organise and negotiate this delicate relationship.

Chapter 7

Culturaid: 'Raising cultural awareness'

A school-based Black history and culture parents' group

Culturaid: Cultural Curriculum Support

Culturaid offers parent-run, school-based support in the form of a parent-led curriculum cultural support role. The curriculum support strategy is designed to enable parents to assist the teachers in developing culturally appropriate curricular experience for their children. In doing so the intention is that the parents become more directly involved in the life of the school and enable the curriculum to have more relevance for the pupils.

Since the focus and conceptualisation of Culturaid was distinctively a collective as a group of Black parents, rather than the support of their individual child, individual case studies will not be adopted.

Brief history

The Culturaid parents' group, set in an East London primary school, has the development of African and Caribbean curriculum materials as the origin of its inception. It began with the head teacher publicising that the school desired to celebrate Black History Month and was seeking support from Black parents who wished to become involved in workshops to create materials for the project. This was, the head teacher reported, due to the humanities co-ordinator trying to 'take on board what the borough was doing and run [their] own Black History Week'. A teacher of Caribbean ancestry from the Local Authority's African Caribbean Achievement Project (hereafter known as ACAP) was attached to the group half a day a week following their bid for support from the Multicultural Support Service. According to the head teacher, the school was 'more inclined to get someone to work in class with the children'. However, the ACAP teacher, together with the humanities co-ordinator and the head teacher, raised the idea of the Black History Workshop which would link around Black History Week and put together curriculum resources which the parents could use in class. The group of mainly African and Caribbean parents has met regularly since then with the routine running and organising of the group being left with the parents and the ACAP teacher. The humanities co-ordinator remained as a link person with oversight of the group. All the parents agreed that the ACAP teacher had an integral role in its weekly sessions but she left for a position in another borough due to the LEA's uncertainty about the availability of 'Section 11' funds. A new ACAP teacher, also of Caribbean ancestry, was allocated to the school. It was this teacher who was present at the weekly sessions during which the researcher observed the thriving group of Black parents, mainly African Caribbean, who met one morning a week in the parents' room at the school.

Contextualisation: ACAP and parental empowerment

This group is one of a number of Black parents' groups throughout the LEA, overseen by the African Caribbean Achievement Project which provided support, staff input and training as part of its remit to encourage the setting up of Black parents' groups within the LEA. Winston, the ACAP team leader, explained that 'all the parents' groups are different'. From his account, they arise out of the perceived needs and interests of the parents at the schools involved, stating, 'some parents' groups just want to come in and do Caribbean evenings or fundraising or whatever'. ACAP has formed an LEA-wide 'Parents' Forum' where members of all the Black and other ethnic minority parents' groups, whatever they choose as their remit, meet regularly.

The rationale of the head teacher

The rationale for the original project, as explained by the head teacher, Harriet, was 'to help raise the profile of Black history in the school and hopefully encourage some parents who don't regularly help in school to come and get involved'.

The rationale of the ACAP team leader/ACAP

The ACAP team leader described the parents as 'role models to the teachers and the children'. Their presence in the school and the type of activities undertaken by what he named 'this powerful group of Black parents' was explained in terms of 'raising the cultural awareness of staff and children, developing a fruitful partnership and ultimately, supporting the learning and achievement of the children'.

Two selections from the ACAP community forum report point to the way that his position reflects central aspects of ACAP's underlying rationale. 'Black Parents feel marginalised and their concerns are often ignored. There is a need for partnership with schools' (p. 2). 'Schools need to focus on raising standards and look for support from parents, community and Black teachers' (p. 3).

The rationale and activities of the parents

Interview data from the parents revealed a key reason for the parents' motivation in getting involved:

> A lot of [people] have very negative views about Black people. Trouble-makers and things like that. And even our Black children don't know that we have Black inventors ... way back ... light bulbs ... and traffic lights ... .
>
> (Parent: group interview)

The role they played was explained by another parent as, 'You're teaching everybody then about your culture, not just the Black children.' They were 'helping the children to learn', said another. The parents and ACAP teacher showed me examples of booklets they had made on Black historical achievers such as Samuel Coleridge Taylor, the UK-born composer; and Latimer, the Black American physicist. They explained that they had made them 'for the teachers to use with the children'. The materials showed creativity and were produced with a high level of professionalism. These included not only the aforementioned books and posters about famous Black people but a wider spectrum of material including a Caribbean cookery book and a Caribbean poetry anthology. I was proudly informed that 'some of these were put in the library' and that teachers regularly use them as part of their work. Certainly, the 'big book' which they had made appeared to be the type of text used by teachers as part of the National Literacy Strategy, and teachers confirmed that they had made use of them in class.

The parents' group did not just make the material but used it in the classroom. This was a surprise for some, as one parent explained: 'I thought we would make the things and the teachers would do it ... would take it from us ... but after we made the project we actually went into the classroom, presented it ourselves, got involved with the children.' Although surprised, their response conveyed pleasure to find that their input extended into the classroom to support the learning of the children. 'We did a story book and we did the props for the story book. We put them in a bag and we actually went into the classroom and did it for the children. They enjoyed it.' Using the stimulus of a published story about a young girl and a quilt, the parents had made a quilt and other props and had facilitated the children producing several pieces of cross-curricular creative work:

> They had to think about the actual process of using their memory ... We also showed them how the quilt was associated with Black people ... How Black people used the quilt in the past by using it as a form of media ... and also mentioning that during slavery times they would use the quilt to send messages to tell the slaves. They hung it up on the line

discreetly, it was a way that wouldn't be obvious to someone just walking past.

(Parent: group interview)

Winston, in his contribution to a group interview, brought out the parents' achievements in the way they had approached the teaching and learning of Black history, especially the subject of slavery. He expressed the view that the manner in which the parents introduced the children to the subject of slavery showed sensitivity and understanding of how to relate such a subject to children of primary age. He argued cogently, for instance, that 'Part of slavery was a resistance to exploitation'. To him, the parents' description to the children of the use slaves made of the quilt was to be interpreted in this context, showing that the role of Black people in history was not merely passive. This was contrasted by the parents' own school experiences:

> We were taught that basically it's slavery and you know if you look back your forefathers were slaves. That's as far as it goes.
>
> (Parent A)
>
> You're lucky you got that. We never got that, We got Henry VIII.
>
> (Parent B)
>
> I wasn't taught [about slavery] and I went to school in the West Indies. I suppose it's a lot to do with it being British ruled as well.
>
> (Parent C)

In considering the original remit of the group, there was consensus from data from all sources that the group had been successful in achieving their aim of bringing Black history to the children. It seemed from the parents' statements that the children had not known of the events and figures prior to the parents' input.

The parents' comments portrayed how keen they were to ensure that their own educational experiences, which had resulted in a lack of knowledge or incomplete picture of the slavery experience, were not duplicated in the way they presented this subject to the children. One pronounced, 'When I was at school I was taught that Black history was slavery and Black history is not slavery. That's a very small part of history in general but it's not Black history.' As adults, a learning outcome of being involved in the parents' group was that they had taught themselves a more accurate picture of the role of slavery in the wider picture of Black history and achievements, and it was this which they wanted to portray and, it would appear, succeeded in portraying. Alongside information about slavery, there was teaching and learning taking place about some Black contribution to science, to the arts and other curriculum areas, providing positive images of Black people. What the parents and others seemed especially pleased about in their claims were improved learning outcomes specifically in relation to their own cultural heritage and improved learning processes more generally in terms of the children's engagement with their schooling. A parent for example related how 'teaching children and the age group that they're at, they'll actually learn and remember so it's nice to be involved at a point that they'll actually keep in the information'.

The parents were able to point to certificates the children had received for participating in some of the events. Despite the potential impact of all of this, nobody made claims about it being reflected in overall attainment measures like SATs results, hence I did not pursue this line of enquiry.

What was discussed, however, was the way in which the parents' input was not confined to their work on Black history. It extended to cross-curricular examples of in-class parental involvement including poetry readings, an illustration being the parent recalling in a group interview, 'remember when Carol did her poem, the grandmother poem, and that went down really well'.

More latterly, the parents informed me that they had been asked by the school link person to organise a community day. After noting some initial reluctance by the group, I saw evidence of them working very hard for several weeks to organise the event. They used some of the sessions, for example, to produce leaflets and other publicity materials. One parent told me how, toward the date of the event, they visited the school 'sometimes two or three times a week'. I attended the Saturday event and was able to make in-depth observations while providing a video recording for our respective uses. Children from many different cultures performed a variety of acts such as playing the piano, dancing calypso, reciting poetry, and song and dance from Greece, Turkey, Ireland and India. Parents ran cultural stalls such as hair plaiting, hand painting and a demonstration of how to wear cultural attire. The local multicultural bookshop was present, with accompanying African drummers, and a variety of food from different cultures was available. Observations highlighted that it was the parents who undertook most of the organising and the work for the event themselves, with the link-person/humanities co-ordinator having a 'directorial' role. On the day, it was two of the parents from the Black parents' group who compered the event, to which the local Mayor had been invited. It seemed from their comments and the way they performed their role that these parents were accustomed to taking part in school assemblies and this was an extension of such activities. The event was very well attended, in fact the tickets were sold out and raised what was termed by a teacher as a 'tidy sum' for the school.

In the final phases of fieldwork, after the community day, the parents returned to the development of curriculum materials. One of their most popular suggestions within the group was making a calendar of Black people, past and present. 'It will be something for the school' was one comment, which was indicative of their general concern. They wanted their contribution to be useful. The parents expressed the hope that once it was produced it would be placed in the school dining hall.

The impact of the support: pupils, teachers, the school and community

'The children love it'

'Well I think the children love it, to have different people coming into their classroom', was one response from a parent. Their contributions revealed that their presence in the classroom impacted beyond the classroom walls. 'Even after, children would say, "I remember you from when you came into class" … and they'll come up to you and say, "you're so and so's mum, aren't you?" On a more individual level in relation to their own children it seemed that both parents and children were proud of their involvement in the school. 'I think it makes them feel really proud 'cos their mums are involved in the school' (group interview). Another parent gave an example of her child wanting to see the books the parents had made, 'again and again'. Examples were given of students who previously had appeared quiet and shy, making contributions in class, in assemblies and on the community day.

Through the reports of the parents and teachers, it was possible to discern multiple levels of the cultural impact of the parents' contribution. One of the parents related the example of a group member taking in fruits originating from the Caribbean for the children to taste.

> You know that a lot of them had never tasted those fruits before and it's the white children, the Asian children, the Black children and it's showing them that you can go back and say to your mum, I tried this fruit the other day mummy, can we get that again … you're teaching everybody then about your culture, not just the Black children.
>
> (Group interview)

'They've gotten results from it as well'

The parents also expressed the view that the teachers appreciated their contribution. 'They've got a lot of enthusiasm for it', said one, and another described the way the teachers talk about the project 'like it was wonderful'. Moreover, they related that the head teacher 'talks really highly of it, as well'. One of the parents represented the achievements of the group in relation to the school: 'They've seen the fruits of our labour and they've gotten results from it as well.'

The comments made by the head teacher in her interview endorsed this view:

We had an excellent response from the parents and the curriculum resources that we had, they have been beautiful and we culminated it in the assembly, the certificates signed by the Chief Education Officer thanking them for their contribution to the school and we had a photo in the local paper and we ended up with some very wonderful resources that we can actually use in class.

The head teacher was clearly delighted with the profile the group's work had imparted to the Chief Education Officer and with the publicity in the local press. While on fieldwork, I was provided with examples from the local press, with photos and reports of activities such as the community day. Having the mayor and mayoress open the community day provided other sources of positive publicity for the school and its work. The increase in parental participation and involvement has, for the head teacher, been an important benefit to the school. The community day was perceived by the head teacher to have been influential in 'widening out' the group of parents from various different cultures who became involved. She mentioned for example that some Turkish children were doing something for the community day. She seemed very happy that four Turkish families came, for, as she explained, 'they do not tend to get involved ... language issues possibly'.

'It's going to be long lasting'

She pointed out in her interview that 'the school does seem to have reached out far more over the last couple of years'. Although she did not specifically state this may have been due, in part, to the work of the Black parents' group or the involvement of ACAP, I was able to ascertain that this period of time coincided with the onset of the involvement of the parents' group. The success of the group does appear to have been influential at school policy level and to have a role in the School Development Plan. As the head teacher explained, 'We have got a parents' policy but we are actually going to review it in the light of what's happened over the last years because it's been so positive.' This is a very important finding. As Winston pointed out to the parents,

You see the impact of the work you do with teachers is that it's going to be long lasting. It's going to be part of a *plan* ... the Educational Development Plan of the school, so that each year they make sure that this element that you're doing is imported.

Facilitating features

'I think all the staff are receptive'

The input in the School Development Plan was consistent with the head teacher's view that 'I am totally committed to getting parents in, so anything that we can do to involve parents and school, I'm there, which is why I'm so thrilled with the success of the workshops'. The commitment of the head teacher for pursuing new and innovative ways of encouraging a broad range of parental involvement in the school is clearly an important factor in the achievement of the group. The head's commitment to getting parents in, and more especially a wide range of parents in, appeared to be part of an organisational 'culture of welcome'. This was recognised in the last Ofsted report prior to the fieldwork (1996), which recognised parental involvement as one of the strengths of the school. As the head says:

> I think all the staff are receptive to having people in the class because it is the culture of the school. Normally, if you say do you want somebody to help, you're in. We have volunteer reading support and we have a granny that helps every week a couple of days and if people are willing to come in they are very very welcome.

The parents seemed to sense that they were 'very very welcome', not just in the parents' room, but in the classrooms where I was able to observe parent volunteers at work.

'Like our second home'

A recurring observation based on group sessions and interviews in the parents' room was how the parents seemed to demonstrate a sense of belonging. One parent even stated, 'This school is like our second home'. Another concurs with this view:

> I'm always here because I help out in my little girl's classroom on a Tuesday afternoon and we walk in and out, we go to the stock room to get things. No one's watching you. You're free, you can come in and do whatever you want, as long as it's to do with the school, obviously.

Field notes from the weekly sessions indicate that the core group of parents visited regularly. However, these extracts may also be viewed as illustrating how parents' sessions had led to some parents having greater involvement in the school. 'No one's watching you' provides an important point of analysis. In conjunction with statements by other parents it would suggest that because they had gradually come to be seen as a regular presence in the school, they felt they were trusted. Likewise, they showed that they did not wish to betray the school's trust, in the use to which they put the school's resources. During the group interviews, unsolicited comments about 'their' parents' room arose from several parents. The parents' room was warm, welcoming and the school funded a regular supply of tea, coffee and biscuits (as much appreciated by the researcher as the parents). There was a photocopier that they could use and enough space for them to make materials. It was also a comfortable place where 'visitors' such as myself could be taken. Having their own base in the form of a parents' room seemed to facilitate a sense of ownership to the school. In keeping with the 'home'-like atmosphere, some of the parents were clearly friends and one mentioned that she 'had met new people'.

'These achieving parents' – 'they were acknowledging what you do'

Being provided with certificates of achievement during a school assembly was clearly appreciated by the group. 'It was really nice to receive it, and to receive it in front of the school and to know that they were acknowledging what you do.' Another explained, 'my little girl gave it to me, I was really tearful, it was really good that'. The LEA multicultural team leader reported how pleased he had been to arrange for the certificates to be given to 'these achieving parents'. This public recognition as a 'reward' for their voluntary contribution was one of the facilitating factors that seemed to contribute to the continued involvement of the parents.

Talent and initiative

From my observation, the internal dynamics of the group worked well to facilitate its success. Some parents, it was revealed, had been friends with at least one other person before joining the group. The group now seemed a cohesive unit. Over a period of time the 'talent and initiative' within the group, as articulated by the ACAP team leader, became evident. Examples of the range of talent within the group include organisational ability, artistic and design experience, IT, culinary and presentation skills. What seemed to be apparent, however, was that they complemented each other in terms of their skills and contributions. They used their different skills in producing the curriculum materials. One, for example, was a very proficient seamstress and used this to sew some of the 'props' of the story bag. Observations of their sessions revealed that, as in any group, some were more quiet and reserved while others more gregarious but over the period of fieldwork it was noted that all had contributed to the group discussions. Upon being asked who was the 'Chair' of the group they were quick to point out that there was no leader. Informally, it would seem, they took different types of leadership roles as the need arose. No one person dominated. It was interesting to note, for example, that they took the decision that two of them, not one, would compere the high-profile public event of the community day.

The ability to use their talents to produce high-quality resources, texts and information in language accessible to primary school children may be considered another source of the group's success. The parents were seen to be effective at individually and collectively generating innovative ideas, and resourceful in their ability to put these ideas into action. The parents' room accommodated much stimulating discussion and it was observed that the parents were not just 'talkers'. I was able to observe that once they had arrived at a decision on a course of action, they planned and worked to achieve the goals they had set themselves.

Emergent themes

'Time is a big thing'

It also emerged that the availability of time was of crucial importance. One parent reported, 'When you're working full time, you're tired. You literally can't come in the morning anyway ... and if you want to do something in the evening, you get home, you've got to cook.' The response from another parent was, 'I don't mind getting involved now 'cos I'm not working because when my first son was at school I was working and I didn't get involved at all but now because I'm not working every free time I have I don't mind putting it into the school.' Its significance was immediately grasped upon: 'I think time is a big thing you know 'cos if you think of all the people in the group. I mean I come on a Thursday because I don't work on a Thursday. I work Monday to Wednesday but if I was working, I would miss out.'

The belief that she would 'miss out' emerged as a phrase which implicitly revealed the value the particular parent felt about her involvement with the group. Likewise, the parent who had not minded using 'every free time' with the school. The impact on the children and the teachers has already been noted. A quite unexpected finding, however, was the myriad of different ways in which being involved in such a group seems to have provided benefits to the parents themselves: 'It's getting to know people', said one.

'We're learning a lot'

The response the parent received perhaps encapsulates the view of the group:

> It's not only that. It's knowing that you're actually helping the children to learn about something they're not learning about [at school]. So it's learning for us too 'cos we're learning a lot about history and things we didn't know about.

'Learning' proved to be a recurring and significant theme within the analysis and the opportunity to learn was seen to be of value for both themselves and their children. 'I thought it was as a good thing to get involved in and something I could learn from as well, 'cos I did learn, you do learn as you go along, and to help the children.' Evidence of their learning was seen to take place over the period of time involved in the fieldwork, particularly in relation to Black history. Initially, their individual responses in group interviews disclosed varying levels of knowledge of this area. One parent, for example, appears to have more historical information imparted from having a relative who had been a teacher in the Caribbean, and another had a keen interest in Black poetry and writers and had contacts with the owners of the local Black bookshop. Gradually, however, individuals, by their input into group sessions, were seen to have learned from each other by sharing their knowledge. By this sharing and using the resources of ACAP to prepare curriculum material for the children and the school, they have added to their own cultural knowledge. Their activity within the group seems, furthermore, to have stimulated desire to learn more, hence one of the parents reported making use of the books of her husband who is very knowledgeable about Black history. By their involvement in the group and with the encouragement of the ACAP team leader, who appears to have a more culturally politicised understanding, the parents seem to have developed their own cultural awareness and understanding of the importance of such knowledge for themselves and of imparting such information to their children. My field notes based on observations record learning on a more implicit level:

> Their close involvement with the life of the school and especially their work in classroom has given them personal insight into the daily educational experiences of their children. They have become more knowledgeable about the curriculum their children encounter and their classroom and school environment.

The agenda of Winston, the ACAP team leader, 'We're supposed to facilitate parents being more involved in what's going on in the school', seems to have been achieved.

'Make sure they link with the Black community'

An interesting juxtaposition of parental involvement in the school and community was presented in Winston's data. He actively supported parental involvement in the form of Culturaid and other Black parents' groups in supporting their children. The support, however, was multidimensional, as indicated in his views expressed in a personal interview; interestingly, not one of the group interviews:

> We are very much there to motivate and support all Black children. They need to know that they are living in a world which is very racist and how to operate and they have to be very successful, they have to get top grades, they have to study together, they have to learn to co-operate

and have study groups and share videos and make sure that they link with the Black community. [Once at University] go back home and get some of their cooking, go to church when they go back home so that they don't lose touch with their own community ... For as someone said, 'If you have a degree that you can't apply to your own community you just have a qualification from your masters'.

Winston's impassioned perspective clearly underpinned his role as ACAP team leader. Parents' groups like Culturaid and the Parents' Forum linked the academic support to the cultural and community support. Some of the values espoused above were being modelled tacitly within the membership of the group. At the same time, the type of discussion above was not overtly mentioned to the parents at Culturaid. In contrast, however, attendance at the Parents' Forum, with some groups who were more actively involved in issues such as challenging exclusions, revealed more of the stance above.

Learning at home

At Culturaid it was learning that was emphasised. As the following comments by Winston expressed, however, the parents were given insights into examining learning from different perspectives:

> We tend to think we can separate what's learning at home. We tend not to value what's learning at home and some of the research shows it's only 10 per cent of the knowledge that young people have they learn at school. The rest is the home, and the church, and the mosque and the temple and the communities.

With this viewpoint, he believed that 'parents are better equipped to support their children's learning in school but also at home'. He urged them to see that previous experience they had was valid and important. For example, on hearing that one had completed work experience as a classroom assistant when she 'didn't get what [she wanted] as a placement at school' and another had been a Sunday School teacher, his response was, 'You've still got those qualities, haven't you'. They were teachers. I was able to observe him emphasising this view by encouraging the parents to share their experiences by presenting a training session to teachers. Their collective reaction was a significant finding in the contrast it provided between their enthusiastic work and their reluctance to participate in Winston's suggestion. Not even the most confident agreed. The content of an analytic memo in this instance referred to an inconclusive stance as to whether this was a self-imposed constraint on their own part in the education process. The following dialogue accords with this interpretation: 'I think the little bit that we're bringing in is OK. As long as our kids are learning, as long as they're getting it from somewhere, it doesn't matter, does it?' Another parent inter-jected, 'to me, as long as they're getting something, I think that's what counts at the end of the day'.

Another interpretation for at least some of the parents was that this was a 'realistic' attitude based on their knowledge or perception of how schools and teachers operate. Paula, for example, one of the most articulate and confident members of the group, a co-compere of the multicultural day show, argued:

> You've got to remember that they are actually qualified to teach and I know that because we have knowledge of a different area, that's fine. But you've got to remember that people are human and if they feel that they're going to be taught by people who're not actually qualified to teach they could actually take that in a funny way ... in the wrong way you know.

The dominant theme arising from the group interview was their sense of the different responsibilities required of parents and teachers.

Emergent themes: Parental gender roles

'He tells her, she brings it all in and we pick it up'

'Different role' may also be representative of another aspect of the findings. One of the 'leaders' within the group revealed that her husband 'knows a lot about the history of St Lucia, has got all these Black books' and had pro-vided a lot of information for her to use within the group. Upon being asked whether he would be prepared to come in and share this information within the group her categorical response was 'you don't stand a chance'. Her explanation was that

> He thinks it's good what we're doing but he just thinks ... they're taking the ... always come and help, come and help ... 'cos in the West Indies parents don't go near the classroom unless ... He's got this old fashioned idea that teachers are there to teach and why should you get involved and me coming in there every day.

Another parent seemed to understand his point of view and did not appear to see what the fuss was about: 'He tells her, she brings it all in and we pick it up, innit.' This same parent explained that although her own husband did not come to the group, he had magazine production skills and had helped to produce some of their publicity material. She also seemed to suggest that they negotiated among themselves the cultural activities they undertook with their children. Her husband, for example, regularly took her daughter to a venue some distance away, for rehearsals to take part in a carnival. She said she was not the slightest bit interested in doing that and 'left that side to him'. The ACAP team leader did not appear to want to take no for an answer, however, and discussed some of ACAP's 'very successful projects looking for Black men as role models in primary schools' and suggested that the husband with the cultural knowledge that they had referred to could at least 'come in like book week and read it out, tell a story ... I'm not talking every week'. The partner seemed alert to his tactic however, responding, 'and then when they come in once ...'.

The future: emergent tensions and emerging possibilities

In the final visit to the school, the meeting revealed the parents initiating among themselves a discussion about the future of the group. Some expressed concern about the response of the senior leadership team following the community day, for example, writing 'UK representation of the food table is limited' with the advice to 'make more effort to teach the traditional European dishes', and 'We need to collect information on a range of cultures e.g. Scottish dancing, Morris dancing'. For the first time, murmurs of discontent were expressed by some of the participants, with one parent explaining, 'We used to have more fun, until all this thing started, we did all that research on famous Black people, then this took over, and now ...'. Another, in discussing the community day, stated, 'They want us to do all *their* work [my italics] and they take all the credit.'

Their discussion on the future of the group included the possibilities for extending the group to a more culturally diverse range of parents, in particular, those from Asian and Indian origin. They had not yet arrived at a consensus but their discussion included the fact that despite the original leaflet produced by the teacher seeking parents for Black history workshops, only one or two 'Asian' parents had ever participated in the group; one who was married to a white British man, and another 'Asian' man who became involved in the community day. None were attending on a regular basis like the Caribbean parents. Their discussion included comments such as whether it was that they did not wish to get involved or that they were not asked, and:

They don't see themselves as Black do they?

If we put Black and Asian history they might come.

I think it should be Asians as well, I mean it's not fair that we're learning about our culture and at the end of the day we've got to learn about their culture as well.

One of the suggestions arising from the above discussion was to make their own leaflet substituting Black with Black and Asian, in the hope that this would attract more Asian parents.

A more pressing concern for the future of the group was that their new ACAP teacher and Winston, the ACAP team leader, would no longer be with them in the new term.

At the time of leaving the research project the ACAP teacher attached to the school had already left for another post and her post was being advertised. Culturaid was provided with a letter about the effects of changes in the funding of the EMAG (Ethnic Minority Achievement Grant). Additionally, the Parents' Forum included a presentation from a Black adviser from another borough entitled 'What parents and governors can do to contribute to a fair and appropriate use of EMAG in relation to meeting the needs of African Caribbean pupils'. The ACAP team leader's post had disappeared within the new structure and he was considering his career options. With Culturaid's LEA report highlighting the race and gender gaps in the levels of educational attainment and rates of exclusions of Black boys, it seems particularly significant that with the demise of ACAP the LEA had not found a way of retaining this highly skilled and knowledgeable 'role model' Black man and the team.

Although the parents seem, to a large extent, to have conducted the work themselves since their ACAP teacher left and certainly from the data seem to possess the necessary skills and experience, they had appreciated the input of the Caribbean teacher and made effective use of the resources of ACAP. The different perspectives of the parents included:

> With this Black history workshop we don't really need anybody to run it, can't we just get on with it, just do it?

> But if we haven't got anyone from ACAP, I don't think they're gonna want us doing it.

The qualities of the parents and the contribution of the ACAP team were both important to the success of Culturaid, according to observations and other data. The school-based ACAP teacher planted the seeds of the idea of the Black history workshops with the head and initiated the work with the parents. Winston, the ACAP team leader, had a broader agenda, as the facilitator of the LEA parents' forum. Implicit in the following comments was acknowledgement that there was a future for the group, with their 'strong, dynamic, creative energy' with or without ACAP's input:

> I have to really motivate the parents. I have to empower them to probe further. When you're in a school like this, the opportunity is there to make an impact on them. If you're making resources for them, then they like that.

> But the parents, they need support, although they are dynamic they need guidance and they need to work with another group to see how

another group operates, they can learn from each other, because some of the groups that are doing other things are not doing this. Networking, sharing ideas and sharing power.

Implications for schools

The parents at Culturaid were delighted that they were 'learning a lot'. The case study provides 'learning a lot' for schools also; particularly those that wish to promote greater involvement of Black families in the life of the school.

Several strategies used by the head teacher offer practical ideas that schools could adopt directly or adapt according to their needs. Using Black History Month as an initial point of focus has clear appeal and would work on a number of levels from one-off sessions to the longer term impact seen at Culturaid.

Whilst Culturaid provides exemplary practice of the way the parents themselves play a key and multi-faceted role at their children's primary school, it is evident that the conditions were to a large extent present to foster their greater commitment. The evidence that the teachers were receptive to parents going into classroom and influencing, shaping and delivering a curriculum with a multicultural dimension shows a level of rapport between teachers and the parents. For schools where constructive relations are not so well established, it might be more appropriate to approach this as a pilot study.

The establishment of an ethos where the school is 'like a second home' has largely been due to the head teacher, who *demonstrates* her commitment to parental involvement. Unlike mobilising parent involvement around Black History Month, ideas such as a dedicated parents' room, including parental involvement as part of the School Improvement Plan, inviting parents to assemblies are not necessarily new, especially in primary schools. It is the approach to these types of activities that is quite innovative. The parents' room offers the parents enhanced facilities and access and parents are not just invited to assemblies as part of the 'audience' or to see their children being rewarded for the work. Here, it is the parents who are receiving certificates.

Providing opportunities for parents to work together and to use their skills for tangible outcomes like making a calendar and books clearly works as a motivating factor to their involvement. This is particularly the case where a school shows that teachers use the material in their everyday work and curriculum such as the use of their 'big books' as part of the national literacy strategy. This is a type of 'partnership in action' where all parties – parents, the school, the pupils and LEA representatives – can 'learn a lot'.

The learning from this case study is not limited to primary schools, although it is acknowledged that primary school pupils may perhaps be more pleased about the presence of their mothers in their classrooms than many adolescent pupils. The head teacher's openness to use the learning experiences provided by the LEA, EMAG team and the group of Black parents, finding creative ways to motivate parents to become involved and rewarding those who do, works across phases.

Implications for the support organisation

If one construes the support organisation in terms of the EMAG team under the auspices of the LEA, there are key points of learning here. It its initial format, it is a practical example of effective partnership at the level of the LEA and schools. Here, the 'top down' advice from the EMAG team that schools celebrate Black History Month and their support to schools in developing parental partnerships are grasped by the schools in their own 'bottom-up' interpretation and action.

Starting from the current position of the school is considered a pragmatic approach. As indicated by Winston, this is likely to bring some benefits to the pupils, parents and school, and is less threatening to the school. The method of encouraging schools to develop their own approach to parents' groups, whilst developing a strategy where a member of the ACAP team is available to them and each parents' group has the opportunity of meeting with groups of a different nature, provided access to best practice and offers a level of indirect challenge to 'improve on previous best'.

A higher level of challenge and support is afforded by the LEA employing someone with an in-depth understanding of the myriad of factors that contribute to supporting Black families to lead a team such as ACAP, as Winston did. On a number of important levels, it assists in the thrust toward raising attainment of African Caribbean pupils, whom national statistics consistently show are underperfoming as a group and over-represented in exclusion statistics.

The impact of more and more funds being devolved to schools, with less funding held centrally by LEAs, means, however, that there are differences across LEAs in the availability of high-quality resources such as the ACAP team. At Culturaid, for example, the team is being dismantled in favour of a more mainstream approach. Whilst schools may be able to 'buy back' some of the services, according to the model used in a particular LEA, having availability of a designated person and team within the LEA is considered a crucial force for facilitating and sustaining projects such as Culturaid. Partnerships of the nature of Culturaid must be encouraged and supported financially if we are serious about 'supporting Black pupils by supporting Black parents'.

Chapter 8

Some conclusions and theoretical insights

This chapter offers an account of the extent to which 'a parent is a parent is a parent', based on a cross-case review of the outcomes of the five examples of organisational support to Black parents in support of their children's schooling and interactions with schools. It will highlight from the parents' perspective their current experiences of home–school relations and involvement with the organisations.

In keeping with my intellectual stance that theorisation is as valid as generalisation to increase understanding of the necessary contexts for improvement in professional practice, the chapter will offer a theorised review of the results. The potential impact of the organisations and the factors involved in facilitating successful meeting of the parents' needs will end this theorised account.

The next section will address the contribution and significance of the study and how this investigation of Black families relates to research and literature on home–school relations in general.

As a researcher, I consider it imperative that the book includes a reflection on the methodological processes and research questions beneficial to fellow researchers and the ever increasing number of classroom practitioners conducting their own research in professional settings. This will end the chapter and will act as a methodological underpinning to the concluding chapter, which offers ideas for professional practice and policy that may move us toward some solutions for supporting Black pupils by supporting Black parents.

To provide coherence and methodological precision to the above, the research questions, mentioned generally in Chapter 1 as part of the background to undertaking the study, are now presented in detail:

1a What is the nature of the provision that each organisation offers African and Caribbean parents in support of their children's education?

b What rationale is given by the organisations for such provision?

c What role has the parents' race played in the group's rationale?

2a What are the needs and expectations of the parents in the cases under study and why are they seeking support in organisational bodies rather than as individuals?
b To what extent are these parents' organisations meeting those needs and expectations?
3a What is the potential impact of such provision on
   i   the families they support?
   ii The nature of home–school relations for such families?
b What factors seem to contribute to the success of the organisations in the provision of assistance for these parents in supporting their children's education?
c What theoretical insights does the study reveal for:
   i   supporting African and Caribbean parents in supporting their children's schooling?
   ii home–school relations for African and Caribbean parents?

In studying the five organisations and gaining a range of data to deepen understanding of the way in which they approach the provision of support to Black parents and their reasons for their particular stance, the parents' voices resonate clearly. Their experiences and narratives leave a powerful effect that refuses to be separated from or become submerged within the study of organisational support as precisely as the construction of the questions above would indicate. In this chapter, therefore, whilst all the research questions are addressed, the outcomes will be discussed in a 'real world' way that provides coherence to the issues emerging from the study, rather than rigidly responding to the questions sequentially. This approach takes account of the interconnected nature of the various strands: the parents' needs and expectations, organisational rationale and provision, the potential impact of different types of organisational provision, and the contributory factors to successful meeting of the parents' needs.

As they really are

Gramsci said, turn your face ... toward things as they exist, now. Not as you would like them to be, not as you think they were ten years ago, not as they're written about in the sacred texts, but as they really are: the contradictory stony ground of the present conjuncture.

(Hall 1989, cited by Clifford 2000: 94)

In the 'present conjuncture' the parents' relationships with their children's schools were not commonly couched in policy terminology of 'partnership', 'home–school agreement' and 'inclusion'. For these parents, the 'stony' terrain of the school grounds is littered with obstacles preventing effective home–school relations. Not having found it possible to work in partnership with schools, their agency is sometimes used to select actively another, less rugged, path leading to the support organisations, in an effort to meet the various needs involved in navigating successful outcomes for their children and their own home–school interaction. 'You have been there for me, you were helping me because there was a need', says one of the parents from Linkaid (p. 42). All the organisations were attempting to respond to the needs of the parents as presented to them.

Aspects of Giroux's work may be drawn upon here: 'Human agency is not subsumed within the logic of domination, it simply chooses the grounds on which it might be operationalised' (Giroux 1983: 167). To the parents' and the organisations' way of rationalising, if their experiences have led them to the view of the school being unreceptive in their practices, it may be more judicious for parents to choose the grounds of parent support organisations, community-based organisations or other support strategies that are quite separate from the school.

'Supporting the need to know'

The 'need to know', as explained in the plea from Mrs Clark (p. 49) at Linkaid, was one pervasive need. The experience of parents like Chamberlain, Clark, Brewster and Wambu who used both Linkaid and Actionaid, the community-based organisation, was that despite teachers, in particular middle and senior leaders within the schools met through Linkaid, expressing the view that the school had provided information for parents about their child's courses, the majority of the parents, on the evidence of their own questions and queries at Actionaid, were clearly unacquainted with the intricacies of coursework, examination and assessment requirements. Parents reported that they were not 'informed early of underachievement', a key recommendation in the list produced by parents after the achievement session at Linkaid (p. 27). The parents I met via Linkaid seemed hungry for information about how their child was doing at school and how they could assist.

It was towards meeting the need to know about the procedures and stages of the exclusions process that Mediaid and Actionaid directed most of their resources. Mediaid produced a video for sale in response to the Chairman's view that 'the parents wanted training about exclusions. They did not understand law and needed information about the basic legal process' (p. 70). Advocaid's training with case studies based on 'real' exclusion cases and an accompanying pack of information about the legislation was in response to a similar need.

'Augmenting parent power'

The organisations, like the parents, were clear that the provision of information was necessary and important to the extent that it may provide the additional confidence of knowing how the education system operates, the types of questions to ask, the issues to raise, the options available to them and their rights as parents. Both parties were equally clear that information by itself was not sufficient to enable the parents to exercise these rights and address all the issues that led to them seeking the support of the organisations. Featured within the organisations' rationale was the use of such information and other strategies as a means of providing an additional source of power to the personal power that the parents had in many cases already attempted to exert in their interactions with schools in trying to support the schooling of their children. Mrs Clark, for example, had become frustrated in her attempts to obtain past examination papers from one of her son's teachers and it was only through my intervention as the Linkaid teacher that this was achieved.

Associated with the need for power was that of protection. The Jamaican proverb 'fowl can't ask hawk to protect chicken', expressed by a participant at an Advocaid workshop (p. 95) is indicative of the view articulated by other parents across the study. It suggests that they could not trust that the school would protect their child's interest or their own as a parent; another source of protection was needed. To increase their parental power and to protect their children's interests some made the most of the opportunities available through the remit of my Linkaid role at the schools. Some wished to avail themselves of services that would provide them with the ability to circumvent the school grounds unless absolutely necessary, such as parents' evening, and still have their needs met, like parents needing quite specific information about school and examination processes. Others, especially those needing support over exclusions, welcomed the ability of Advocaid not only to explain the processes involved but to walk with them, across the school grounds and into any meetings with governors or an LEA appeals panel. What is significant is that, in attempting to look after the interests of their children, all the parents were motivated by a belief that engaging with schools on an individual basis, was not, by itself, meeting their needs and expectations and that it was through organisational engagement they were likely to have more of an effect, to exert more *power*.

'Especially Black parents'

The imbalance of power which served to preclude a partnership approach in home–school relations was one of the key themes linking writing about parents in general and Black parents in particular in the literature reviewed in Chapter 2. Likewise, recent government websites (DfES 2004a, 2003) and leaflets with information about the education system appear to demonstrate an acknowledgement at policy level that parents 'need to know' this information. What the data from the organisations and parents in this study seem to be suggesting, however, is that asymmetrical power relations, a lack of a partnership approach and information about school-based processes are likely, for *race-related* reasons, to have a negative impact on 'especially Black parents'.

The documentation of Mediaid, Linkaid and Actionaid and the rationale for their provision referred to the under-representation of Black children in terms of academic attainment. All of the organisations included in their literature or interviews the statistical over-representation of Black boys in exclusion. Recurring as a theme within the explanation for being in contact with the organisations was the parents' view that schools were failing to help their children educationally, as explained in Pablo's concern for his son that 'they're failing him as a student' (p. 68).

The whole remit of the home–school liaison role was to intervene in this process by promoting pupils' achievement and the 'active involvement of African and Caribbean parents'. A barrier to both was what the parents experienced as a negative attitude toward them. Mediaid referred to 'common cultural stereotypes' (p. 62) and that 'cultural difference and racial disadvantage are central to the exclusion of Black pupils' (p. 74). Even within Culturaid, the organisation with the most positive relations with their children's schools, a major rationale for their being involved was the 'very negative views about Black people' that a lot of people have (p. 112). At Actionaid, even some who did not wish the group to focus on racism as an issue expressed the view that 'we know that racism is preventing Black children from achieving, especially in a place like Actford' (p. 53). Advocaid, however, was more explicit in its view that, at some schools, 'children experience the same kind of oppression and racist practices as adults in the wider community (p. 95). 'As they really are' from the organisations and parents perspective, the school grounds have additional, race-related obstacles, hence the path to home–school liaison is experienced as especially stony and unwelcoming for 'especially Black parents'. It is within this context that the parents underscored Mrs. Clark's view that 'especially Black parents, they do need to know' (p. 49) and that the participants enthusiastically responded to the comment that 'fowl can't ask hawk to protect chicken' (p. 95).

Potential protection against underachievement was offered by those organisations working with the children through, for example, school-based mentoring and providing support with study skills to help the young people themselves develop strategies by which they could focus on their academic studies. Mediaid's home- and school- based pastoral work and Linkaid's mentoring activities with Black students from the local university may be interpreted in this proactive manner. Similarly, the more preventative work being undertaken by Advocaid in its conference workshops was designed to provide the parents with the necessary information about the education system and some strategies to undertake their own advocacy role as Black parents.

The need for power and protection, in conjunction with the information on offer, was particularly acute for those facing exclusion panels; Josette's panic (p. 84) Maureen crying (p. 90) and Edward reporting how 'they're shaming you' (p. 98) may be contrasted with their sense of empowerment through working with Advocaid. Edward for instance, states 'the school was not expecting the fight we gave them ... you become more willing to fight back through contact with Advocaid' (p. 106). Sandra believed it was the combination of knowledge about the education process and knowing 'powerful' members of a group like Advocaid that was influential in the school deciding not to exclude her brother (p. 94). She was also clear that having their representation placed her in a more powerful position than as an individual parent. The need for a more powerful ally was particularly important in circumstances where the parents considered they needed to challenge schools. In the face of what was experienced by some of the parents as racist or discriminatory treatment by some teachers, the organisations were a potential source of protection where their individual efforts at 'going through the right channels' had met with little response.

In practice, the actions of the organisations and the parents exemplify, in Gramscian terms, what Mercer termed the 'uneven' nature of the process of power and resistance within hegemonic relations referred to in Chapter 2. (p. 15). Drawing on Gramsci's concept of hegemony, the parents, like the personnel within the organisations, appear not ready to accept the beliefs and norms about Black children and families or ideological explanations about Black educational outcomes that appear to be deeply embedded within the schools. The work of the organisations and the parents' use of them portray their agency in resisting and struggling to claim successful outcomes for their children as well as equality and respect. The more grass-roots type of organisation, like Actionaid, or the more independent organisations, may also contain manifestations of the phenomenon described by hooks, a Black American feminist, whereby:

> Within Black culture, a counter system emerged that was counter-hegemonic, that challenged notions of individualism ... Black folk created in marginal spaces a world of community and collectivity where resources were shared.
>
> (1989: 76)

Whilst this might have become, over the years, a less frequent phenomenon in some contexts than 'how things really are', it is within this theoretical framework that Winston's philosophy behind the LEA parents' groups may be viewed. They were, he said, 'there to motivate and support all Black children'. He was aware that 'they need to know that they are living in a world that is very racist and how to operate and they have to be very successful. They have to get top grades' (p. 120). This stance, however, was within a framework of 'cultural co-operation' where the type of activities he was espousing to achieve this end challenged notions of individualism: 'They have to study together, they have to learn to co-operate and have study groups and share videos and make sure that they link with the Black community' (pp. 120–121).

In theorising the 'real world' that Black parents and children inhabit, the parents expressed awareness of the need for supporting their child's pursuit of the best credentials they were able to achieve. Michelle, for example, explained that 'It's hard because they have to do so much more. Because although it could be Trevor and a white boy for a job, same qualifications but they would find something and give the white boy at the end of the day' (p. 86). Mrs Clark reasoned that 'you do need to push your child more and you need to be on top of them more because it's so much harder ... Where a white person can go and get a job you've got to have three times the amount of qualifications to even get to that position' (p. 24).

Theoretically, the individual interests were to be combined with the collective. Agency was to be combined with awareness of structural constraints. In theoretical terms, the 'powerful group of Black parents' (p. 111) forming Culturaid, together with the influence of the ACAP team and Winston's leadership, had created a 'marginal space' of 'community and collectivity'. In a culturally co-operative framework, Winston's intention was to link that group with other Black parents' groups in the LEA in order to undertake 'networking, sharing ideas and sharing power' (p. 125). This was a view articulated by Pablo, a parent at Mediaid: 'It's one thing to have communication between schools and parents but it's also important that we have communication between each other because then you build community' (p. 70).

The concepts of building community, sharing ideas and sharing power that emerged from the study have led me to incorporate aspects of the concept of social capital. Social capital embodies networks built on concepts such as trust, shared goals and shared values (Coleman 1990). Drawing on this theoretical concept, the parents of Culturaid, by using their own social capital, were developing reciprocal relationships with each other and with the school so that all parties were 'learning a lot'.

The philosophy behind Culturaid, and Perry's view that 'we need to understand our roots and culture', suggest that one form of social capital that could usefully be deployed by Black parents is a global knowledge of Black history and culture and pride in cultural identity. For those parents with a cultural grounding, this may contribute to the development of social capital that can then be passed on to their offspring, similar to the economic and cultural capital transmitted by some. It may possibly also act as a protective factor against the phenomenon described by a parent at an Actionaid workshop: 'It's difficult for Black children growing up because the things that are projected about Black people on the whole are negative and when you fit into a European perspective of who you're supposed to be that creates problems ... you're supposed to be failing' (p. 51). Similarly, Pablo's comment that Black boys are 'almost expected to fail' (p. 68).

The organisations had a role to play in developing different aspects of social capital. Key to this was 'sharing our perspective' and inter-generational knowledge. At Linkaid and Actionaid, a combination of Black teachers and mentors worked together with the parents to provide potent social capital networks, building on the cultural resources within the communities. The commitment of volunteers at Mediaid and Advocaid was considered to be fundamental to the success of the organisations. The pastoral work of Perry at Mediaid, for example, was particularly helpful in supporting families with Black boys who had been identified as at risk of underachieving. Likewise, Yvonne working with girls such as Teresa.

The result embodies Epstein and Sanders' conceptualisation in 'Connecting Home, School, and Community: New Directions for Social Research' (2000):

> The results of interaction between family, school and community members are accumulated and stored as social capital ... social capital [is] increased when well-designed partnerships enable families, educators and others in the community to interact in productive ways.
>
> (Epstein and Sanders 2000: 288–289)

It could be argued that rather than taking a 'new direction', 'especially Black parents' have traditionally been motivated to incorporate social capital within their cultural framework, with a long established cultural knowledge that 'it takes a community to raise a child' and use of resources like supplementary schools. Parents such as Claudette reported, 'I'm a single parent, I haven't got my family, my large family here. My parents are back home' (in Jamaica) (p. 106). Those living in Actford, where 'Black people are used to sticking out' (p. 37) or in –shire 'where you see one Black person in a year if you're lucky' (p. 93) welcomed the cultural social cohesion resulting from their group sessions where, in a 'helpful, kind and different environment' (p. 55) they could address issues related to 'especially Black parents' (p. 49).

The ideology of professionalism

The present conjuncture for the Black families in the study does not tend to resemble a picture of 'connecting home, school and community' embodied in the general theoretical conceptualisation of social capital. The 'ideology of professionalism' may help to provide some illumination:

Mac an Ghaill's (1988) chapter is particularly relevant since it is a classic text within its specific focus on 'student–teacher relations in the schooling of black youth'. In his theoretical interpretation:

Ideologies work within a common educational paradigm, with a set of shared assumptions from which emerge certain issues that are defined as problems. Of primary importance is the teachers' shared perception of the Black community itself as constituting the problem in the schooling of Black students.

(1988: 38)

If one examines, in theoretical terms, a 'de-racialised discourse', Maclure suggests that teachers' identity claims 'can be seen as a form of *argument* as devices for justifying, explaining and making sense of one's conduct, career, values and circumstances' (1993: 316). In this theorisation, teachers' expectations of 'appropriate' parental behaviour and home–school relations would be framed by a concept of schooling and partnership within their ideology of professionalism. To adherents of this ideology, the argument that those parents who cannot or choose not to work in partnership on these terms are seen to be at fault, rather than the practice within the institutions themselves, appears 'justifiable.' Likewise, attempts at challenging the cultural practices of school, either by parents or pupils, are not embodied within the ideology of professionalism.

The cases brought to the organisations suggest that when a racialised dimension is factored into the equation of power dynamics and the ideology of professionalism, the potential for conflict is accentuated. The view that some boys were in need of a male teacher to 'look at their attitude to white authority' (p. 32) written by a head teacher at a Linkaid school is recalled here. Not only is it indicative of an expectation of automatic deference to teachers as authority figures but also the specific reference to white authority contains explicit ideological messages of a relationship built on cultural superiority. Deference to authority in general and a deference to white authority in particular is what seems, from the words used by the head teacher, to be expected of both parents and their children.

From the parents' viewpoint, however, deference as parents was not always an appropriate option if they were to protect their child's interests. 'Safeguarding our children' (p. 93) was the title of Advocaid's case study report. 'Without a shadow of doubt, that head teacher was racist', was how Edward (p. 101) described the former head teacher of his son's school and again, of the teachers, 'I feel that they resented the fact that they were dealing with inner city kids, with predominantly Black kids' (p. 102). From some parents' and pupils' perspective, and not just those whose children had been involved in the exclusions process, the teachers' actions were not fulfilling the role of those who should be expected to behave in a 'professional' manner. The view of Mrs Clark was 'it was like talking to school kids to be honest with you, in one ear and out the other (p. 50). Another parent, Mrs Chamberlain, demonstrated a similar response to the teachers as her son: 'He's not going to respect them just because they're teachers. He feels it's got to be earned with intelligence and ability to teach' (p. 21). Respect rather than deference to professional authority was what was being promulgated by the family and it was a respect that was earned by behaving in a professional manner.

Sandra, having attended an Advocaid training programme, set up a lone parents' group, 'giving the parents that sort of empowerment that, yeah, although teachers are professionals, they don't have the ultimate control of what happens to your children' (p. 98). A participant at the conference workshop gave similar advice: 'institutionalised racism, that's a long term thing and we continue to fight that every day but what we *can* do as parents is take an active stance. Make sure that we attend not just parents' evenings but if there's an issue, don't take things as gospel' (p. 101: italics added). The schools' response to the parents' agency was to perceive their actions, like that of their children, as the parents having 'an attitude to white authority'. This is indicative of Blair's point, in her study of school exclusion and Black youth where she explains that 'Accusations of racism, implying an intention to hurt in some way, violate teachers' sense of themselves as people and as professionals' (2001: 10).

The Linkaid and other data revealed parallels between parents and children where power was a negative attribute in their hands: 'A very bright lad, very able, feels he's been picked on by some of the staff, Mum a very powerful lady, hot on rights, feels it's racist (p. 33). The same teacher, referring to another pupil, states 'a very powerful boy, a very big body' (p. 33).

Whilst this type of power tended to result more in overtly conflicting situations with boys, it was not only boys whose perceived power may be interpreted as a challenge. Davinia was described as 'difficult, mum's a powerful lady and will support her (p. 34) and another was 'quite powerful for her group of friends' (p. 34). It is consistent with Maclure's insight that when this power was used to support a teacher's 'ideology of professionalism' to serve the teacher's interests, as in 'in class … she tells off kids who aren't listening', Davinia was described as 'more sensible' (p. 34).

The data across the sets would suggest that a school's narrow cultural expectations in terms of behaviour of both parents and children tended to act as a major barrier to the legitimate academic aspirations of Black students and their parents.

The partnership within Culturaid suggests there may be some room to manoeuvre in the way the ideology of professionalism is interpreted and this may have benefits in fostering a school culture conducive to effective relations. The head teacher appeared not to be overly concerned with overt displays of power and control and there was mutual respect. Additionally, there was an openness to finding out about the different cultures, to try a range of approaches to encourage parental participation and to learn from the parents. Fundamental to the effectiveness of the group was that the parents were trusted to work among themselves and make decisions with the minimum of input from the head teacher or school. In making these theoretical constructions, however, the fact that Culturaid was the only group that was based at a primary school may be important. All the staff being 'receptive to having people in' (p. 117) may be more likely to be part of the culture of some but not all primary schools and was a facilitating factor in the description that 'this school is like our second home' (p. 117).

The parents forming Culturaid provided improved learning outcomes to teachers as well as students, specifically in relation to their cultural heritage and the multicultural agenda which they, the parents, have espoused, and also improved learning processes more generally in terms of the children's engagement with their schooling without directly facilitating a formal training session for the teachers, as was the initial suggestion. They had made an impact whilst seemingly leaving the teachers' ideology of professionalism intact by indicating their awareness that 'if they [the teachers] feel that they're going to be taught by people who're not qualified to teach they could actually take that in a funny way' (p. 122). The political consciousness of the two ACAP teachers, with Winston as the team leader, when combined with knowledge and understanding of the ideology of professionalism was also crucial. Winston was clear that through being at the school, the parents had the opportunity to make an impact and both he and other ACAP teachers used their cultural knowledge and professional credibility to indirectly influence the outcome.

The potential power and protection afforded by the organisational stance adopted

In theorising the role of the support organisations and the factors that appear to contribute to their 'success' in meeting the needs of the families, it is important to address questions about the potential impact of the stance they take to parental support.

The feature common to all five organisations is their recognition of the futility, at this stage, of challenging the ideology of professionalism *overtly*. Linkaid and Culturaid worked within this framework. Mediaid's initial 'softly softly' non-confrontational approach (p. 62) was indicative of their general stance to the mediation role they attempt to adopt. It is only when we reach the boundaries of professional control, to the semi-legal questions of whether schools do or do not have a right to exclude, that Advocaid and latterly Mediaid feel that it is useful to challenge overtly the authority of the school. Recognition of this feature is important in considering the future impact of the organisations and the different stance they take, supporting the families and on the nature of home–school relations. The organisations, like the parents, recognised the 'limits and possibilities inherent in different sites'. Actionaid kept away from the terrain of the school altogether, in order that there could be openness and honesty. What, therefore, Actionaid was able to do that Linkaid could not, in its school-based provision, was to allow a frank discussion between the parents regarding some of the 'under the carpet' (p. 49) information requested by the parents in trying to support their child's academic attainment. However, Linkaid was to some extent able to support parents' desire for knowledge about their child's progress through the insider position in the school and its classrooms.

Mediaid and Linkaid, as well as Culturaid, engage with schools in a manner with a view to influencing schools through attempts at shared problem solving but were aware of the constraints such as those associated with the self-serving, ideology of professionalism; or that, 'you have to remember that you're working for the school' (p. 40). Advocaid, however, tends to be in a position ostensibly of winners and losers, with only one winner possible. They are aware of the effects of power dynamics and the need of the parents for protection against arbitrary use of power, hence they explicitly state whose 'side' they are on. Whilst this may to an extent be seen to be leaving the school unchallenged in respects other than exclusions, they are, in terms of their understanding of the situation, making the only decision capable of providing the necessary protection. It is because they and all parties are clear about the boundaries of their provision that Advocaid was considered by the parents to be so supportive in the particular situation of exclusions.

The findings would suggest that it is the more independent support organisations that are the most able to provide parents who use them with protection and a form of that which Lareau (1989) terms 'home advantage' cited in Chapter 2 (p. 17) and which, drawing on the Bourdieuan theoretical framework, she suggests that middle-class white parents possess due to cultural capital. It is perhaps for this reason that the organisations, apart from Culturaid, seem to have been most valued by parents when they supported them on terrain apart from the school, and that the parents at Linkaid insisted that the Actionaid group should not be on school premises.

The effects of being an organisation specifically intended to address the needs of Black parents would seem to intensify the possibility of schools feeling threatened. This clearly had implications for the way in which the organisations were able to operate. What seemed to be implied from the study was that explicit mention of racism, as with the Advocaid stance, was likely to be interpreted by some schools as suggesting that individual schools and teachers were racist and to be met with hostility or at the very least defensiveness. My Linkaid work in schools at the time suggested that teachers were, having been influenced by the Macpherson report and the Race Relations (Amendment) Act, beginning to address notions of institutional racism but were not often able, even the most 'liberal' of them, to consider that any of their own personal practices to children and parents were capable, intentionally or otherwise, of having the outcome of disadvantaging certain groups of students more than others, or indeed, of being construed as racist. In stark contrast, the findings from the organisations and parents was that in order to be effective, issues of race and culture had to be addressed.

Pablo's poignant plea is recalled here, 'when education fails us and society fails us, when our parents fail us because they can't understand what's happening in society, where do we turn?' He is asking 'if there's one organisation' to meet the parents needs (p. 70). The results from the study would indicate that 'in the present conjuncture', different organisations, with clearly defined remits and strategies, may, by different routes, be able to offer the 'support from knowledgeable people' that Pablo, and the study as a whole, suggest that 'our children and parents need'.

In some circumstances, especially situations that may require an *overt* challenge to the ideology of professionalism, like exclusions, 'characterised by a gross imbalance of power' (p. 83), it may not be feasible for one organisation to provide both knowledge and protection. Other types of organisation may, however, through adopting a more 'softly softly' approach help to support the 'need to know'. Culturaid, Actionaid and Mediaid provide information on Black history, Linkaid and Mediaid help the need to know about pupil progress and what is happening in the child's class, Linkaid prioritises school processes, and Actionaid offers strategies for supporting their child's academic attainment.

For some parents, however, even the organisational support they had tried was not considered sufficient in terms of either power or protection. They then actively select other routes. One parent, Aduah (p. 89), decided to send her son 'back home'. Others turned to the path leading to what may be theoretically considered one of hooks' 'marginal spaces'– a Black-run school. Claudette and Maureen (p. 104) considered this better at meeting their child's needs. Maureen reported that her son had achieved his examination results there. Claudette found the teachers more receptive to Black parents than other schools where they 'didn't listen to you'. 'I prefer the teachers here. They're kind and they understand ... I don't know if it's because they're Black or what' (p. 104).

Contribution and significance of the study

In theorising the experiences of the families and the organisations supporting them, to some extent their interaction with schools is as would be predicted by Bourdieu's theories. The findings about the schools' lack of understanding and devaluation of the assertive attitudes or indeed commitment to educational outcomes of Black children and their parents are all associated with what is regarded as cultural capital. However, where it would seem that my findings are not consistent with the above and with Bourdieu's theory, or indeed conflict theory in general, especially as expounded by twentieth-century theorists such as Gramsci and Althusser, is the readiness of these Black parents to reject the ideological position of schools which implicitly asserts that the only culture of value is that of the 'dominant' groups within society. What the parents, irrespective of social class, do instead, however, is to engage in exactly the kind of resistance and struggles that theorists such as Gramsci thought to be necessary. Black women and men of different social classes and economic backgrounds were leading and working in these organisations.

Fierce dedication and willingness to challenge are the types of parent power manifested by participants in the study at all levels of the social strata. Such challenge was not necessarily in an overtly conflicting manner, for example efforts by parents such as Pablo 'not to aggravate the situation' (p. 68) and the parents forming the Culturaid show. Neither was it a stance imbued with automatic deference. Crozier (2000), however, has pointed out class differences with regard to the white British population. Working-class parents of her study, whilst very committed to their children's education, tended, in contrast to middle-class groups, to be more deferential towards the professionalism of teachers and less likely to intervene in the schooling process.

Social class and parental power

> You're looked on, you're judged, by the way you dress, the way you speak and as a consequence your child now is judged. If the parent doesn't look tidy they think the child can't *think* straight. It's a misconception but that's how schools are generally.
>
> (p. 68)

As discussed in Chapter 2, the common conceptualisation within the more general literature and theoretical framework on home–school relations is that being a middle-class parent brings cultural advantages due to schools awarding recognition, indeed approval, to middle-class culture which is seen as congruent with the aims and values of schools. Middle-class parents are perceived as literally and metaphorically 'speaking the same language'. However, notwithstanding Pablo's view that 'Black parents in shirts and ties, they've been treated differently', what reports from Carmen and other Black middle-class parents reveal is that, for Black parents, their profession or social class is less of a factor than their 'race' or culture, in the perception of the school. The salient finding about the resemblance in the experiences of both middle-class and working-class Black parents would concur with a previous article by Crozier, this time focusing on a case study of 'knowledgeable' Black parents, where she argues that 'in spite of having the advantage of educational knowledge and awareness, there is a dissonance between the parents and the school' (1996: 253). The findings from this study should help toward understanding of the nature, extent and reasons for the dissonance as well as strategies the parents adopt and those that teachers may consider for developing cultural co-operation rather than cultural exclusion.

The above discussion portrays part of Callender's 'new' perspective to research. In the field of home–school relations the findings have been shown to add to the neglected body of literature of Black researchers who have investigated these issues in the past and those who have brought important fresh insights using their knowledge of these Black communities. Written by a Black researcher, about the contemporary UK experience of parenting in relation to supporting the education of Black children, the study offers significant new contributions which reveal that whilst some of the aspects of home–school relations for Black parents are connected with the more general issues of being parents, there are other aspects that are specifically related to being parents of Black, in this case African and Caribbean, children. In meeting all these needs, the findings suggest that the 'Black Education Movement' (Tomlinson 1985) and Bryan *et al.* (1985) may have been given a contemporary resonance with support organisations such as some of those within the study.

In tandem with the literature of Black researchers, Tomlinson has proved particularly relevant to this study, for she is in a powerful position in the field of home–school relations and Black communities since she has investigated and written in depth on both the 'old' (1985) and the 'new' (2000) disadvantages faced by Black parents. She argues that parents of minority ethnic children have become increasingly aware of the need for academic credentials and has highlighted that 'the failure of the education system to deliver equal access and educational success to many minority children remains a source of considerable tension' (2000: 18). 'Remains' is a crucial word here. The findings to an extent reveal somewhat of an indictment of educational institutions in the way in which the energies of these Black parents and Black communities continue to have to be employed to counter some of the very same disadvantages discussed in Chapter 1, that Tomlinson and some Black educationists were writing about in 1985 and previously (Coard 1971; Stone 1981). Moreover, the 'new disadvantages' compound their effect. These include impediments highlighted in interviews with parents which corroborate Tomlinson's appraisal of the way in which policies such as 'school choice' have had a disproportionately negative effect on the Black communities. The publications of Advocaid echo the suggestion of Munn that some schools may be choosing parents rather than vice versa (1993). Bryan's assertion that 'it is *racism* which has determined the schools we can attend and the quality of education we receive' may, from the views of the organisations and the parents, be perceived as more likely now than when she wrote in 1985.

This study confirms what Claudette Williams (1995), in her study of Black parents described earlier, termed the 'fierce dedication' with which

Black mothers support their child's education. In addition, whilst Black mothers were heavily involved, some Black fathers were also undertaking support strategies. It was also more complex than the white British feminist body of research portrays. As Aduah's case revealed, although she was separated from her husband who was not living at home, her son saw him every day and her husband was supportive. Moreover, they had made a mutual decision not to have him come with her to meetings with the school. Other parents, for example Edward of Advocaid and Pablo of Mediaid, were among some of the most overtly active in their interactions to try to support their children's education.

The various insights which this study has generated have helped toward the development of a theoretical perspective to reflect the culturally specific experiences of African and Caribbean parents in their relationship with schools as well as their more general experiences as parents and the various strategies adopted to support their children's education. Second, by drawing inductively from the specific stance taken by the five parent support organisations, the study has developed theoretical understanding of the kinds of circumstances in which various methods adopted by organisations wishing to support Black parents are more likely to be effective, and the potential impact of these organisations on the parent, child and school.

Reflection on methodological processes

The research strategy has proved advantageous in obtaining detailed information in response to questions from both strands of the research area of interest: analysis of five cases of organisational support for African and Caribbean parents, and the parents' experiences of home–school relations leading to the need for such support. Considering the outcomes of this project the decision to use a multiple in-depth case study of the organisations has proved beneficial. First, it has, as intended, afforded the opportunity to test the initial impression of diversity of approach to support among the organisations, and provided a wider evidence base for the conclusions reached. Within the case study of the organisations, the presentation of the complete cases has exemplified the different way in which the five organisations work with individual parents. In adopting a different research position in each case, however, whilst being a professional and pragmatic decision to maximise the research opportunities available, the ability to make cross-case *empirical* comparisons has been to some extent diminished due to the impact my different position may have had at each case. However, given the wealth of information and understanding gleaned through the different stance taken, and the emphasis on theoretical generation rather than empirical generalisations, the professional judgement is that this was an appropriate decision. I was always aware, nonetheless, that the various roles adopted at the different organisations required me to be sensitive to the data generated in the different cases in order to make an informed assessment of the factors that were found to be important. Likewise, the concentration on parent support organisations rather than schools is considered appropriate in affording the opportunity to study, in a new and in-depth manner, the nature of home–school relations for the families supported by them.

Ethics and positionality: whose side did you say you were on?

The ethical decisions were more varied, complex and complicated than anticipated. Analysis of reflective memos reveals that most of the ethical issues were concerned with decisions about the use of information revealed by the participants. This was particularly problematic in the action research role as home–school liaison teacher at Linkaid, and especially with the families involved in Actionaid, the community-based parents' support group. The monthly meetings were interspersed with informal conversations with individual parents, social gatherings and telephone calls. As a researcher, to what extent I should include the type of information, sometimes very personal, was a major concern. This was compounded by knowing that in such a small community it would be difficult to camouflage identities.

In undertaking an assessment of the differential impact of the various aspects of my identity on the research project, the conclusion is that it was the cultural credibility as an aware Black person which was of the most benefit in enabling me to maximise the benefits of research training and skills. My gender is also considered to have been a factor, although possibly less so. Like Williams (1995), Callender (1997) and other Black researchers cited, it is possible that the parents, many of whom were women, may have been more willing to discuss these matters more fully with another Black woman through our position of what Williams has termed 'insider researchers'. As in Bhatti's research (1999), the parents felt comfortable enough to adopt the vernacular at times. Unlike some of the teachers, I understood their language, the cultural codes and conventions. It is believed that on a very basic level, a researcher without this first-hand cultural insight may have missed some of the finer nuances of the meaning in the data through a lack of comprehension. For example, none of the white British teachers at a training session I facilitated on home–school liaison with African and Caribbean families were able to ascertain the meaning of an example of Caribbean dialect used by a parent. A more profound methodological effect was, however, that across the socio-economic spectrum the parents had judged correctly that I was able to understand some of their experiences as a Black person living in this country. This cultural credibility and understanding enhanced my research skills and knowledge, by facilitating an extra dimension of trust and rapport that I was able to develop with the parents, hence enhancing the quality of the data obtained.

As a researcher, an interesting methodological finding was the way in which the parents were able to distinguish between my professional *knowledge* as a teacher and my *role*, especially at Actionaid, where I was involved in setting up strategies to meet their needs as parents of Black children. This may be compared to my own attempts to reconcile the needs of the research project, the parents and their children, the organisations and the home–school liaison role. The fact that the research strategy was to examine organisations aimed at supporting parents in support of their children's education had led me to place more emphasis on my identity as a Black community worker than as a former member of a senior leadership team, in the perspective I took. In principle, I could have taken a more reserved stance in relation to the parents but that would have pragmatically been unhelpful and I might have been, in principle, uncomfortable. In the home–school liaison role at Actdale I discerned that the relationship with some but not all of the teachers became more guarded as I became more involved with the parents. In spite of this, I was able to elicit direct information from some parents and to exercise tangible but not necessarily overt action. It could be argued that making the decision to extend the home–school liaison role outside the confines of the school and to the community may, to an extent, be construed as being prepared to be perceived as having taken the side of the parents. In the second school however, with a culture that was more open, a more co-operative relationship was maintained. For instance, I supplied the school with leaflets about the mentoring scheme and mentors from the university were linked with pupils.

The processes, problems and choices have been discussed with a critical awareness of the methodological consequences of the fact that, in qualitative research, 'the researcher is the research instrument' (Hammersley 1997: 3). As the research instrument it is the researcher who is open to scrutiny. It may also be the case that 'equality' or 'race-related' research may be open to particular scrutiny including potential charges of being 'unobjective' or 'political'. Foster *et al.* (1996, 1997) have criticised some researchers of inequalities of 'race' and gender, on the basis that they 'over interpret' the data in arriving at explanations for inequality such as racism. I have discussed these issues in a previous article (Cork 2001a). I would point out here, however, that in reflecting on the methodological approach to the analysis of findings relating to racism, one of the factors that needs to be explicitly addressed here is the nature of the word 'racism'. The word itself arouses strong emotions. As the facilitator of training at Actionaid found: 'it's one of those issues.' The approach adopted focused on how, as a researcher, I understood the participants to be using the word racism and investigating the experiences and circumstances in which they use the term. This was intended to be useful in enabling me to appraise the common-sense understandings emerging inductively from the language of the parents and teachers in the light of other evidence and themes, including those of theory and background literature, and to make connections and develop more complex theoretical structures to aid understanding of the issues involved and explain persuasively the experiences and perceptions of racism of the participants.

Like the nature of the word 'racism', the nature of research studies into 'equality', 'underachievement' and/or 'race related' issues needs to be explicitly addressed. Lord Swann's posthumously published chapter outlining his work on 'Education for All' explains how such studies deal 'with something quite different, namely, sensitive social and political problems which are inherently far more difficult, and where objective evidence and guidance is much harder to come' (1993: 1). Notwithstanding that 'objective evidence' is itself a problematic concept, it is considered important to mention some of the methodological features and aids to credibility that have been used.

Briefly, a range of systematic steps were taken to enhance the methodological credibility of the research project. Field notes were systematically maintained, for example, and throughout the record-keeping process I differentiated those words that were actually spoken by the participants from my own comments on them, in the reflexive, analytical memos. Examples of evidence from the parents and personnel of the organisations were cross-validated with each other and with evidence from other sources, including documentary evidence from the schools. 'Quality control' of the validity of the data included using the very helpful guides provided by Seale in *The Quality of Qualitative Research* (1999: 189–191) and Edwards (2002). Full details of methodological matters may be obtained from the doctoral thesis on which this book is based (Cork 2001c). At this stage, however, it is being pointed out that a range of strategies and 'quality control' measures were used in respect to methodological accountability. They enable me to possess the methodological confidence to be able to state that the findings depict important themes that have emerged from the data, for which I am able to offer methodological confirmation.

Chapter 9

Steps toward solutions

Implications for schools' practice and policy

Cultural co-operation or cultural exclusion?

Implications for schools

Together, the case studies paint a comprehensive, detailed, fully textured and unfortunately somewhat bleak picture of how these parents' expectations of schools and teachers were unrealised. This wide array of data portrays powerfully how their own motivation as parents seems to have been left untapped, in a similar manner to the academic potential of their children. What is valuable, however, are the insights into the lived realities of home–school relations from the parents' perspective.

As a first step in moving toward solutions, it is recommended that schools seek to obtain the views of parents on the 'lived realities' of relations between their own school and Black families. In seeking their views, since we have already established that there are issues for 'especially Black parents', race-specific questions would need to be posed alongside the more general questions with an emphasis on finding out, from their perspective, their expectations of the school. The focus here is on using qualitative data because of its potential for eliciting the type of powerful and convincing responses seen within this book. The intention is that this would sit alongside the kind of statistical data analysis that schools and LEAs tend to undertake on a more general basis, and audit tools such as 'Learning for All' produced by the Commission for Racial Equality.

If the 'present conjuncture' is that baseline data in some LEAs show that when African and Caribbean students make the journey from home to primary school they achieve among the highest results, yet by the time of results at aged 16, they are attaining among the lowest results (Gillborn and Mirza: 2000), it seems no longer tenable that schools can continue to leave their own processes unexamined.

The current shift toward self-evaluation at all levels from schools to LEAs provides important opportunities for schools to conduct meaningful monitoring and evaluation of the impact of all their processes. Ongoing systematic monitoring of school policies, practices and outcomes according to race and gender as part of *standard* procedures, embedded within the School Development Plan, as the work of Culturaid was, may alert schools early to ways in which they may directly or indirectly be affecting particular racial, socio-economic or gender groups. Salient examples from the study include the manner in which generic strategies on raising attainment of 'underachieving groups' and involving more parents of this group left 'equality gaps' in provision for girls and gifted and talented pupils within the generic group of African and Caribbean pupils and their families. Information from monitoring and evaluation may alert schools to such 'equality gaps' and may then be used to actively seek strategies, in and out of school, including community-based organisations such as Mediaid and Actionaid, to assist schools with the process of targeted improvement.

A key feature of cultural co-operation is recognised by Lorrayne, the volunteer at Advocaid: 'you're respected in what you do and your way of life'. As part of the process of self-evaluation, schools may need to consider the extent to which their curriculum, indeed their whole school culture and way of interaction, demonstrates visibly to the families that they are 'respected'.

This book contains key points of learning for individual teachers. It emerged quite clearly that, unlike the teachers whose names frequently arose in negative terms by Black families, those teachers who appeared to have more positive relations with parents and children were less likely to expect an automatic deference to their authority and to focus less on displays of hierarchical power. In Hall's neo-Gramscian 'contradictory' world, they were also the most likely to receive the respect of students and their parents and to facilitate learning. Iris and the Head of Year at Actmount school are clear examples.

In contrast, the case studies depict how conflicting relations that parents and pupils have with a school tend to converge around specific teachers and suggest that individual teachers can erect considerable barriers to 'cultural co-operation'. This may take the form of racism or acts of discrimination against individuals, or more covert manifestations of general cultural stereotyping of both parents and pupils and concentrating on aspects other than a child's intellectual aptitude. Any solutions for supporting Black pupils by supporting Black parents would need to take into consideration the need for their 'protection' against this occurrence, both on an individual and on a wider institutional basis.

The concept of 'protection' used by parents at both Linkaid and Advocaid provides a useful angle with which to view the needs of Black parents and to seek solutions which reflect those needs. Protection against potential underattainment, protection against an external environment that parents have themselves experienced as racist and may, their experience suggests, discriminate against their children even when they have qualifications, was a fundamental requirement. In the eyes of the parents, it should be a school's duty to provide such protection. Schools cannot solve the global problems of discrimination in the external environment. Schools can, however, take steps to ensure that the pupils and parents do not need protection from a hostile *school* environment, one that appears to exclude pupils without due regard to principles of justice, or one that denies them the opportunity to maximise their academic credentials.

The implementation of strategies with a clear focus on achievement is one such step. It is likely to motivate 'especially Black parents' since it provides protection against their children joining the dismal statistics of academic failure, hence the success of the achievement session and the workshops at Actionaid. In seeking solutions, schools may need to consider how to find appropriate 'helpful, kind and different' ways of offering such protection. Forums that provide avenues for 'people to bring along their problems' (p. 54), to gain information about what they 'need to know' to support their children's learning, or perhaps to produce 'culturally specific' curriculum material, for instance about Black achievers, are all types of interventions that schools may offer to promote such an environment.

It is salutary for schools to note that in the absence of this type of environment, some of the parents were seeking to send their children to a 'Black-run' school. Like 'Syble's successful children' in a chapter by McCalla (2003b) (albeit in a pre-school context), this setting facilitated success for pupils and parents. Others sent their child 'back home'. They recognised when 'common cultural stereotypes' were being reinforced by schools, either about them as parents or about their children, and how this may impact on the pupils' chances of academic success.

The experiences of parents, including Aduah above as an 'unmarried African woman' who believed she was stereotyped because of this, and Pablo, so motivated to support his children, offer key pointers when seeking solutions to improve relations between schools and Black families. A lack of knowledge of the circumstance of these families, or misinterpretation of aspects of their culture, had a profound impact on pupil achievement and presented barriers to their involvement with the school. On a fundamental level it also led to schools failing to recognise when these very parents could help to facilitate some of the solutions to issues. Pablo is just such a parent. Potentially, the school could have encouraged Pablo to train as a learning mentor or teaching assistant as a graduated approach to building up confidence to become a teacher. Someone such as Pablo would have made an excellent teacher in general and role model to young Black boys. Given that schools and policy (e.g. DfES 2003; TTA 2000) constantly reiterate the need to recruit more Black teachers and that it is now possible to become accredited as a teacher through school-based routes, this is one avenue that should not be overlooked. Even if not recruited into teaching, schools could proactively seek to involve fathers such as Pablo and Edward in working toward solutions, especially but not necessarily exclusively in relation to supporting Black boys.

The situation regarding Black boys is indeed critical and well recognised. (Sewell and Majors 2001; Sewell 1997). The London Development Agency (2004) adds to the literature by reporting that in 2003, 70 per cent of African and Caribbean boys in London left school with fewer than five GCSEs at the top grade of A* to C or equivalent, while African Caribbean men are the least likely of any group to have a degree. Their experiences, as depicted within the LDA report, concur with those in this book, for example, 'the boys complain of racism and stereotyping'. In this study, we were shown how the parents, as well as the boys – and girls – experience 'racism and stereotyping'.

The challenge and complexity of trying to unravel some of the issues and move beyond these to constructive solutions are recognised within the book. With the support of Black fathers and Black mothers, schools would be better able to distinguish those issues which may be related to the teaching and learning of boys in general terms and those which may be related to Black boys in particular and African and Caribbean boys more specifically. We may, for example, examine Lorrayne's comment about the difference in attempting to support her two daughters and her son (p. 103) and Edward's views about the way in which schools differentially treat his daughter and son 'right through to examination level and then leaving school' (p. 68).

At school level, the study suggests, like Blair's research (Blair 2001 38), that despite the challenges, individual schools, with strong leadership of the head teacher, can shape their culture in ways that are more likely to result in a partnership between parents and the school. As Linkaid's case study revealed, the skills of classroom teaching, of *improving teaching and learning*, are not mutually exclusive from taking significant notice of what one may be able to learn about the children from parents, or indeed from the pupils.

Creative approaches to the provision of opportunities within the classroom and the school for pupils to voice their views was not only more likely to facilitate learning but could contribute to 'developing dialogue about teaching and learning' (Arnot *et al.* 2004) that may help in raising attainment. Where the voices of the pupils emerge in the book they provide a pupil perspective on policies on personalised learning, for example, and on pedagogical issues in relation to pupils as independent learners. This accords with the findings of Arnot *et al.* The pupils, like the parents, appreciated classroom and school settings that were 'helpful, kind and different'.

I am not negating the potential for conflict in considering the above as a means towards solutions. Nonetheless, the findings by other researchers (Majors 2001; Gillborn 1990) and from this study would suggest that conflicting relations are already present for many African and Caribbean students, particularly but not exclusively boys, and are a contributory factor to the disproportionate rate of school exclusions for these students and for their continued academic underattainment (LDA, 2004; Bourne *et al.* 1994; Wright, 1987).

It is necessary to point out here that the parents were aware that their children could display behaviour that was challenging. They knew that their child could be 'wilful' and 'how a teacher can be frustrated'. Some acknowledged also that, 'It's easy to blame other people. He [the child]'s got to take responsibility, take his part.' As parents, they were prepared to support a school whose decisions were seen to be just. Unfortunately, for these parents, their experience led them to consider that for 'especially Black children' this was not something they could assume was the case. They were therefore aware of the dangers of always taking the school's word as 'gospel'.

A valuable statement in relation to improving school policy and practice is the comment of a parent that, 'They let you know when your child has been rude but not when your child is underachieving, especially Black children'. It was considered that the stress schools placed on what was sometimes regarded as 'petty' aspects of behaviour was disproportionate to a school's concern about learning aspects.

An associated issue, which has implications for school policy development and practice, is that for some schools, it was at points of crisis for the school and when the school was at the point of excluding a child, or the parent was appealing against a decision to exclude, that the school produced 'a dossier' of complaints about behaviour, with the incidents 'sometimes going back years'. A closer connection between the academic and pastoral staff of the school, with clear direction from school leaders at all levels and form tutors, may assist in improving these practices. The role of Head of Year is crucial here.

This book appreciates the pressures that some schools may be under. A parent points out, for example, that the records about pupils from primary school did not arrive at secondary school in time to cater appropriately for a child's learning and behavioural needs. Furthermore, parents and Advocaid have alluded to the possibility that when schools are placed in 'special measures', exclusions may be viewed as a 'quick fix'. For a variety of reasons, which this study has illuminated, Black students, particularly Black boys, are disproportionately targeted, and are likely to end at a Pupil Referral Unit rather than another school.

Longer term approaches to seeking solutions are more likely to have a sustainable impact on improving home–school liaison with Black parents and on securing the educational attainment of their children. Such approaches, as presented within the book, would include relationship building with pupils and parents, looking behind the 'mask' of some of the Black boys and inspiring trust and confidence, and investigating creative strategies to develop a shared understanding of expectations of the different roles of the parent, child and school.

The study recognises that the job we are asking the teacher to do, like that of the parents in this study, is a highly complex and demanding one.

Motivating and educating young people across the cultural and socio-economic spectrum, preparing them to be principled and responsible citizens of a diverse society, using their talents for personal and societal benefits, are aspects that cannot be attained by one party alone. Cultural co-operation between parents, school and local communities is a difficult but very necessary route to achieving these goals.

Often, however, the co-operation appeared to be a one-directional process. The schools seemed to require that the families co-operate with their policies and practices irrespective of whether they were construed as being prejudicial to the interests of their child or even racist in effect. In policy terms a partnership between home and school is presented as a power-neutral concept. However, as the study revealed, power relations were crucial. A precursor to cultural co-operation is a conceptualisation of the teacher's professional role where co-operation is seen as a two-way process, with the child at the centre; an approach which is aware that irrespective of whether they are a lone parent or married, or of their economic background, parents on the whole want their child to succeed and would co-operate with schools to achieve this.

In turn, the structures, the policies, the practices of the schools, local and central government would need to be reviewed and where necessary changed to show evidence of welcoming such co-operation. In advocating this stance, I am aware, like Walker and Maclure, that 'parent–teacher discourse is quite resistant to change' (2001: 3).

In the study, the parents needed to know that they could *trust* the teachers to educate their child to the maximum potential and to operate their policies in a manner which was transparently fair and free from racial bias. Some wanted to know that if teachers committed the types of racially discriminatory actions against their child for which in employment there may be procedures and sanctions, then similar procedures and potential sanctions should apply. In the 'present conjuncture' the starting point for any 'home–school agreement' would be to focus 'more on schooling than on discipline'; on consensus, not conflict. This perspective on cultural co-operation may be necessary for 'especially Black parents' where 'powerful' and intelligent Black parents and children were seen to be excluded, both literally and metaphorically. It is revealing that it was the voluntary work that Lorrayne undertook with Advocaid, not the school itself, that gave her the confidence and motivation to apply for a school governorship position.

Perhaps the most significant implication for schools seeking solutions is that they may be neglecting their most valuable resource by not finding ways of harnessing the 'fierce dedication' to education demonstrated by these Black parents and the community organisations. An attitudinal shift is necessary which does not view this as adding to their workload but as supporting teachers, potentially, in what should and, at the risk of being considered idealistic, could, be a shared goal: quality teaching and learning, in a constructive, equitable environment where pupils achieve their optimum potential. Given the damning statistics of underattainment and exclusions of African and Caribbean pupils, it may be necessary for some schools to prioritise building relations with 'especially Black parents'.

Implications for the support organisations

Within the organisations themselves the implications of 'especially Black parents' are seen most potently at Advocaid. The positive implications were most likely to be expressed by the families, many of whom seemed relieved that at last they were in a situation whereby they were speaking to people who understood their experiences as Black parents and young persons. The organisation's unequivocal anti-racist stance and avowal that it was there 'for the child' and the family was a major contributory factor to the families feeling supported, irrespective of the outcome. However, the effects of being an organisation specifically intended to address the needs of Black parents would seem to intensify the possibility of schools feeling defensive and threatened. This clearly had implications for the way in which the organisation was able to operate.

The potential impact of the organisations and their different stances

The organisations have all to some degree achieved their aims of supporting the parents in their interaction with schools. This has been most evident in the data relating to parents at the particularly vulnerable period when their child is in the process of exclusion from school. The implication is that, without the organisations' support, school governors and staff merely 'rubber stamp' decisions (Gillborn 1995).

The staff of Advocaid have taken on board the threat perceived by schools about organisations which present themselves at the school or LEA representing the parents and have chosen not to involve themselves in any other school-based links. In contrast, Mediaid was the most explicit in being considered a 'bridge-builder' working in partnership with the schools and the LEA. It was noted that a Mediaid type of organisation made the conscious decision not to undertake any advocacy work as they did not believe that this could be combined with their work in schools. Indeed, as reported earlier, the co-ordinator informed me that she passed those cases over to Advocaid. The attempts by Mediaid to undertake both seemed, in the first instance, to suggest that a likely consequence is that support of parents in relation to exclusions advocacy might be weakened. Some of the parents interviewed certainly expressed disappointment that the organisation did not seem to be supportive of them, their dissatisfaction resulting in them seeking the services of Advocaid. Mediaid has since taken steps to address this by a less 'softly

softly' stance in relation to exclusions, whilst still undertaking a mediation type role in and out of schools. The passage of time will reveal the effects on their partnership arrangements of their less 'softly softly' stance in the employment of a trained barrister. The implications for some organisations seem to be centred on their position. Could they serve the interests of both the parents and schools? This feature was accentuated in the case of Linkaid where the liaison teacher was paid by the LEA and was expected to take a neutral stance in general but where conflicts of interests occurred, the professional expectation was that, ultimately, one's allegiance lay with the school.

To be fully effective, an element of autonomy was seen to be required. For those organisations seeking to maintain an independent stance in relation to supporting Black parents, the financial implications were especially pertinent. It seemed necessary for their source of finance to be separate from schools and LEAs. The head of Mediaid expressed the belief that it was possible to be paid by schools and LEAs for their services and accept funding from agencies such as the police and judicial system without consequences for their ability to challenge when necessary.

In considering the future of organisations such as Culturaid and Linkaid, one of the factors emerging as important was that the government changes to funding mechanisms, in particular EMAG (DfES 2004a) and increasing devolvement to schools, may potentially leave such groups financially vulnerable whilst some schools may not be using the funding strictly for the purpose it was intended.

The more financially independent 'grass-roots' type of group would need to either have or develop skills in raising funds on a national or even international level or be able to avail themselves of support for effective fundraising. Without this, the likelihood is that their work would in the worst scenario be unsustainable or in any event their ability to devote sufficient time to supporting parents may be affected. Cultural co-operation by funding sources and the voluntary sector is another implication of this. What the organisations seem to be suggesting is that even with the potential for securing capital to provide culturally specific support that the various new funding streams appear to offer, they are disadvantaged in terms of 'the need to know', in particular about completing some of the more complex funding bids and by differential power relations.

The HMSO report *Capacity Building and Infrastructure Framework for the Voluntary and Community Sector* (2004) may provide some steps in the right direction for the community-based organisations. Currently, however, like the Black parents in relation to the schools, the Black voluntary organisations' relationship with voluntary agencies and those with the power to award funding demonstrated an unequal balance of power and lack of a Black presence or cultural co-operation. This highlights the need for continued support in views expressed by the National Institute of Adult Continuing Education (NIACE):

By supporting the self-organization of black parents, through resource allocation and other types of support, we can begin to move towards a position whereby black parents' needs are addressed in a more holistic way and that they are enabled to become more active and effective.

(1997: 21)

In discussing the potential impact of the organisations, it is noted that their stance to supporting Black parents varied according to specific local circumstances. One example is the implications of the cultural demographics in the locality of the organisation. For Actionaid, it was observed that the effects of being in a cultural minority where, as Chamberlain said, 'Black people are just used to sticking out' impacted on the parents, teachers and pupils. Any strategies by an organisation would need to take this into account. Organisations' response to supporting 'especially Black parents' required a contextualised approach. It is not appropriate to transfer completely the support strategies from one locality, especially one from an urban more culturally diverse area, to another such as the locality of Actionaid, even though the effect on their children was similar. They were underachieving to a greater extent than other cultural groups in their locality and the rate of exclusion was higher.

Implications for policy

The research on which this book is based illustrates its agreement with one of the recommendations of the OECD review of Educational Research in England; namely, that 'more research would simultaneously address issues of practice or policy and issues of fundamental knowledge' (BERA 2003: 25).

Through the evidence from the case studies we gather the 'fundamental knowledge' that for benefits of government policy on 'supporting families' or 'parental involvement' to accrue to African and Caribbean families, the more generic features of policy in connection with improving home–school relations would need to be allied to a more culturally responsive approach. An apt example is the recent very detailed research-based DfES policy report entitled *The Impact of Parental Involvement, Parental Support and Family Education On Pupil Achievement and Adjustment: A Literature Review* (Desforges with Abouchaar/DfES 2003). Its main strength is that it offers comprehensive information and analysis about various types of parental involvement. It espouses engaging all parents in a proactive way that values their contributions and it points out the need for a school–community basis for such collaboration. Nonetheless, although a chapter on ethnicity is included, the literature or even the chapter itself would benefit from reflecting how 'Black parents over the years have campaigned for better education for their children ... have tried to influence policy and practice' (Blair 2001: 28), or more importantly, *why* they continue in this vein.

This book includes an array of information from the culturally distinctive perspective of the parents and organisations, that would be of benefit to policy makers in supplying them with information that they 'need to know' to improve both policy and practice in supporting Black families. Policies that directly or indirectly impact on the Black families in the study in relation to support of their children's schooling include those concerned with Qualifications and Assessment; the National Curriculum; Gifted and Talented provision; Behaviour Improvement Programmes; Exclusions; School Admissions and Pupil Referral Units.

Policies in connection with the use of funding were also found to impact on Black families. 'Parental and community engagement' is mentioned in DfES (2004a) guidance in the use of the Ethnic Minority Achievement Grant, with case studies of good practice. The parents and organisations would agree with the guidance within the document that 'LEAs and schools should be looking strategically at how all of their resources are used to support the needs of all of their pupils and how, over time, achievement gaps can be closed' (DfES 2004a: 2). A suggestion for policy is that, where necessary, intervention at DfES level may need to be stronger than 'guidance', for instance the DfES documents on exclusions from schools and pupil referral units, and in ensuring that an appropriate amount of the funding is used on strategies to close equality gaps for African and Caribbean families and that their needs are not neglected by funds being channelled into other areas, or being used chiefly to support EAL (English as an Additional Language) issues.

One useful contribution of this book is to show how policy at local and national levels, with the intent of raising attainment and improving schools, may have somewhat contradictory consequences for Black parents and pupils. Advocaid noted how some schools exclude more pupils after being placed in an Ofsted category of Special Measures, as previously described. At the other end of the school-based process, government policy increasingly espouses the notion of greater 'school choice', whereas 'school choice' was somewhat of an oxymoron to some of the parents in this study, particularly in the cases where there was intense competition for places at a particular school.

A policy recommendation is that the DfES, Ofsted and LEAs enhance their current data collection to include the type of ethnic and gender specific statistical analysis conducted by Advocaid. The Pupil Level Annual School Census has already proved to be a powerful analytical tool in this vein. What is being suggested is an extension to this approach that would support Black parents' and community organisations' 'need to know' about issues of concern. These include: applications for school places; exclusions from schools; the proportion of families appealing against decisions on school places and on exclusions and the outcomes of appeals on both. Incorporated would be the statistics on the proportion of Black pupils allocated to Pupil Referral Units and on the exclusion rates of schools in different Ofsted categories. A (2004b) DfES research report, 'Minority

Ethnic Exclusions and the Race Relations (Amendment)', revealed that 'none of the Ofsted inspection reports for the twelve LEAs discussed disproportionality in minority ethnic exclusions.

Undertaking such monitoring and analysis and making the results transparent is recommended at the highest level of policy, since it would send strong messages of commitment that go beyond mere compliance with the Race Relations (Amendment) Act (2000) to a determination to improve target areas. The Audit Commission (2004) reports, for example, that 'delivering improved services to local communities requires determined action to recruit and retain minority ethnic staff. Such staff, with the relevant knowledge and commitment, should help in providing a more responsive service, both generally and culturally. Key policy makers and government services promote the need for a more diverse workforce. By starting from their own organisation, they could model their expectations of others. It seems an ideal juncture for public services to make use of the self-evaluation toolkit provided with the report by the Audit Commission on *The Journey to Race Equality: delivering improved services to local communities* (2004).

Cultural unawareness was a barrier to cultural co-operation that was observed regularly in the study. This ranged from insufficient knowledge of language and customs to the lack of knowledge of the daily lives of the families and the local community. A 'colour blind' approach ignored the discrimination and racism faced by parents and children of African and Caribbean origin both inside and outside of school. The studies would support the view that 'self-evaluation' without more external scrutiny, where the 'self' is culturally unaware, culturally misinformed, or implicitly or explicitly contributing to racist practices, is insufficient.

The impact of any audits and actions is likely to be even more effective if policy makers incorporate parent and community involvement from the initial stages of formulation of policy to any actions proposed as a result of the analysis, review and changes made. Consultation, such as that conducted on the Government's *Aiming High* programme (DfES 2003) to raise attainment of minority ethnic groups, acknowledges the important role of Black parents and community groups and provides illustrations of good practice in a range of areas. *Aiming High* shows scope for further development of partnership working with policy makers, LEAs, schools, parents and local communities. One possibility would be to provide dedicated teams of knowledgeable people, to include those with the professional knowledge and personal qualities of Winston in ACAP and Iris at Linkaid. Working in schools and communities, in order not to be marginalised as in previous models, they would need the financial resources, power and influence to offer support to the various partners at all levels; to be in a position to effect change; and, where appropriate, to be part of the process of challenge.

One of the thorniest issues for policy is in the realm of challenging practices that consistently fail to deliver an adequate service to Black families, whilst ostensibly appearing 'successful'. The type of recommendations I am making, if promoted at the highest levels of government policy, for instance the DfES, may bolster the influence of the LEAs in providing a higher level of challenge, intervention and support to schools where appropriate. They may also require finding tangible ways of rewarding those schools for additional success factors such as actively engaging different groups of parents, high attainment and progress to higher education for groups where statistically this has traditionally not been the case, and schools that manage to maintain low rates of exclusions. Advocaid argues for a 'nil exclusions policy'. Realistically, however, it is accepted that there are situations when exclusions are a necessary course of action, to protect others and the excluded student.

New approaches to policy and practice show potential for supporting Black pupils by supporting Black families. The Children Act (2004), based on the Green Paper 'Every Child Matters' (2003), has co-operation between different agencies at its heart. This may indicate the potential for enhanced links between education and social services fostering a greater network of support and inter-agency working where organisations 'learn from each other' like at Culturaid, and pupils and families benefit. They would, however, be more likely to benefit if these services had a sufficiently diverse pool of staff to fully understand and meet the needs of the Black families. If not, and they all shared a similar cultural reference point, the situation could be compounded. The devolution agenda of services intended to meet localised needs may also have some scope for improvements in services delivery to Black communities, especially if they are part of the various stages in the process. To be effective, potential barriers when attempting partnerships between different professional cultures, for example teachers, education social workers, education psychologists and LEA officers would also need to be addressed at the onset.

It's in your paper policy, designed by you, for you, not me.

(A. Cork 2000)

In considering partnership arrangements with African and Caribbean families, the above extract from the poem 'It's in the Way' (A. Cork 2000) highlights the need for Epstein's consideration of 'well-designed partnerships'. If the perception or the reality is that such partnerships are 'designed by you, for you, not me', this does not embody the principles, practice, or potential benefits of building social capital networks. From the perspective of the parents, the effect is then likely to be that of a 'paper policy', a cosmetic exercise.

The opportunities available from the government's recent commitment, including financial commitment to partnerships with local communities at the centre, suggests fruitful possibilities. In particular, in some of the funding streams is an underlying assumption of rearrangement of power relations where, instead of the schools inviting parents to the table (Hulsebosch, 2000) the possibility is that the community organisations may be inviting schools to the table.

A significant example is the annual series of very successful conferences on 'The Education of the Black Child', organised mainly for the Black community, with Diane Abbott MP, a Black woman, at the helm. It invites key policy makers (rather than schools) to make a contribution whilst at the same time challenging policy with hard-hitting reports and recommendations including some proposals for reducing exclusions. Examples of major partnerships it has developed include one with the London Development Agency which set up an Education Commission to help meet their concerns, and a partnership with the GTC (General Teaching Council) for a network of support for Black teachers and governors.

A book of this nature cannot address all the issues in supporting Black pupils by supporting Black families. It was made clear at the onset that it is African and Caribbean families that are at the centre of this study and the reasons should be more understandable through the evidence gleaned from the case studies. It is not suggested that other groups may not have some similarity of experiences. McIntyre et al. writing on 'ethnic minority' students more generally, have argued that 'It is the area of developing more effective communication and collaboration between the homes and schools of minority ethnic students that initiatives beyond the schools themselves would seem to be most needed' (1993: 31). Also, Bhatti (1999) has published an ethnographic study which has an insightful portrayal of Asian children at home and at schools. The more generic features of parental involvement dominate the research agenda and policy, however, as depicted in the DfES (2004a) review of literature in this area. Citing Cummings, a statement from the forward-looking book Learning without Limits has some applicability to generic policy: 'The "generic student" whom trainee teachers are prepared to educate is "white, middle-class, monolingual and monocultural' (Hart et al 2004).

In this comparatively rare book on the experiences of contemporary African and Caribbean families in the UK, I have focused on the families' experiences and those of the organisations attempting to support them. Given the small-scale nature of the study, I have not differentiated between the experiences of African families as distinct from Caribbean families. There is scope for exploration of this, although the report by the LDA (2004) has indicated that, for London schools, the difference may be slight. The study has a host of implications for parents that have been alluded to in the book and to do them justice they should be more fully discussed in another text specifically catered to an audience of parents. In this book, I have prioritised the implications for schools and for policies.

A report by the Joseph Rowntree Foundation (2004) reveals that racialised experiences and racism are prevalent and persistent in the provision of services. One area of comparative international research that would be quite valuable is to examine home–school relations for Black parents where 'race' and 'racism' are not so embedded societally. Parental involvement and home–school–community liaison is, for instance, equally high on the policy agenda of several countries where many of the families of UK pupils originate, for instance, from Jamaica and other parts of the Carribean and from parts of Africa. In such a context, one may be able to 'tease out' those issues that are pertinent to families and to effective parental involvement, and any cultural issues, in a situation where the families are not an 'ethnic minority' within a country. In seeking solutions from this international perspective, one may therefore concentrate on understanding and developing key factors emerging within this book such as strategies for sharing information on what parents and teachers 'need to know' to fully support the children's education. Education policy makers and practitioners in both countries should gain from sharing perspectives and methods, as would the families. A further international research area, that surfaced from the experiences of Chamberlain and his family, is the possible usefulness of exploring further some of the approaches that the US adopts to these issues in comparison with the UK.

The case studies of Chamberlain and Brewster point to another key area for further research: the educational experiences of parents with children of mixed heritage. 'The present conjuncture' reveals that families with mixed racial heritage are a growing phenomenon. (Alibhai-Brown 2001; Tikly *et al.* 2004). Home–school relations of families with pupils of mixed racial ancestry does, from the findings, seem to be an area worthy of further investigation. Given the small selection presented, and that this was a feature that emerged unexpectedly from the Linkaid role at the school, their needs were reported under the general focus of 'especially Black parents' whilst attempting to portray some of their experiences, especially in the complex and contradictory ways in which the schools responded to them.

There is a definite 'need to know' about and understand issues of culture in this area if we are to provide appropriate strategies of support to parents with children of mixed heritage. I will not offer any comments of a more general nature at this stage. I will instead agree with the cautionary note provided by Boushel (1997) that 'in current professional ideologies ... the complex experiences of these children and their parents are often ignored or conceptualised in a very simplistic way'. Whilst there has recently been a valuable research report entitled *Understanding the Educational Needs of Mixed Heritage Pupils*, the needs of the parents are not its main focus. The contribution of this book includes some parents with children of mixed heritage. More usually, as Tikly *et al.* (2004) have pointed out, they are 'invisible' in school and policy discourse. This book has recognised that their needs are more diverse than would be met by being totally encompassed within strategies for Black parents. It would appear that, in addition to a specific focus on strategies for families with pupils of 'mixed heritage' as a group where one of the parents is Black (for example African, Caribbean or African–American ancestry) they may also benefit from some of the strategies for 'especially Black parents'.

In considering the future of these organisations for the support of Black parents and the improvement of home–school relations, the findings contain the tensions and contradictions that are almost inevitable in a 'real-world' context. These were implicitly associated with the various routes the organisations and parents take and the extent to which either a bridge can be built across the terrain or the obstacles circumvented, challenged or removed. This study is not presented therefore as a simple and uncomplicated panacea of 'what works'. Instead, through the study of five organisations and the groups of parents seeking their support, we become more aware of what was seen to work in the different contexts, what did not work, and the conditions which may be necessary for the different types of support organisations or home–school interaction to work. This point is especially important when one considers implications for policy.

The OECD states: 'Researchers must accept that the results of traditional individual university researchers working on a self-defined small-scale research project is unlikely to influence policy and practice in education' (OECD 2002). The intention, however, is that results of this interpretive, smaller scale research are intended to sit alongside studies of 'what works' and those with a broader and more statistical evidence base, such as that provided by the more 'generic' research-based report by Desforges with Abouchaar for the DfES (2003). A reminder is also being made here that the research on which this book is based is combined with the writer's practitioner and policy experience.

To untangle the deep-rooted and complex 'social' and 'political' issues surrounding Black underachievement, and to consider the role of Black parents and support organisations in intervening in this process, space must be claimed within a democratic research agenda for 'culturally competent' researchers' 'self-definition' of research questions, issues, approaches and indeed solutions, with members of Black communities. Some of this research will unavoidably have a 'critical edge'. Practitioners, the research community and policy makers will need to foster an environment in which 'difficult' questions may be pursued. However 'difficult' they are, especially where claims of racism are made, these are the conditions that have the potential to lead to solutions offering more credibility with different 'communities' and increased likelihood of success in involving all parents and in 'Raising the Attainment of Minority Ethnic Groups'.

This book reinforces the issue that in supporting African and Caribbean parents, the cultural components of parental support need to be integrated with the challenges faced by parents in general in the complexities of contemporary society. In a newspaper article comparing the time forty years ago in this country when his Jamaican-born mother undertook a personal challenge to educational authorities to protect the educational interests of her child, Muir writes, 'It is clear that the need for black parents to take a protective stance towards their children is, if anything, more urgent today than it was then' (Muir 2004: 23). The findings within this book would certainly concur.

In this text we have delved behind the headlines and uncovered a myriad of ways in which Black parents from all levels of social class continue to challenge for better educational outcomes for their sons and daughters, the reasons why they challenge, and how they may be supported in their aims. We have shown, moreover, that in 'the present conjuncture' the organisations and parents are still of the view that 'fowl can't ask hawk to protect chicken'. Advocaid, on its own terrain, and some aspects of the work of Mediaid, continue to be needed and used to offer such protection, especially in cases of exclusion. Actionaid works to protect against underachievement and other issues, on a site separate from the schools.

Despite the challenge, which is not to be underestimated, the work of Culturaid, and aspects of the work of Mediaid and Linkaid, would seem to indicate that there is potential for some cultural co-operation providing information and strategies for parents, teachers and young persons to 'focus more on schooling than on discipline'. Those parents are not advocating that schools should ignore matters of discipline, but are seeking a shift of emphasis. They knew that they had a part to play. Some for example prioritised parents' evening, despite a hectic round of commitments including 'studying too' but found them as unhelpful as some of the teachers in meeting their 'need to know' about issues other than behaviour.

It is important to note that, similar to the parents, the work of some of the organisations contained elements to support schools over behavioural issues. It seemed to them, however, that a school was at fault if it focused 'more on behaviour than on learning'. Telling examples include a school where a gifted and talented child could not move up into a higher set until the school considered his behaviour had improved, and where the behaviour of another teacher was such that a pupil who generally behaved well did not want to go up a set to avoid being in her class. In seeking solutions, the parents and organisations would wish for these types of scenario to be investigated and remedied, if we really are 'aiming high'.

'Teachers and their unions want to work with the African Caribbean Community – pupils, teachers and parents – in tackling an issue which is long overdue. But this has to be done in a spirit of partnership, not blame' (NUT 2004). There is indeed a role for professional associations, including the NUT, as part of the solutions. Partnership, however, as seen, and as Osula (2004) has discussed, is not unproblematic. Equally, through this research-based examination of different methods of supporting Black pupils by supporting Black parents, we are led to understand why the arguments start and why blame is apportioned when considering these serious, disturbing and long-standing issues. We appreciate also the urgent need to move forward, beyond 'paper policies', beyond any rhetoric of 'partnership' and 'equality', toward substantial and sustainable solutions at school, policy and community level. This book, from a Black British perspective, will certainly add to the debates, arguments and theories. It could also contribute some of the solutions.

Bibliography

African Caribbean Attainment Project (1997) *Community Forum Report: Building Effective Partnerships Between Parents – School – Community*, London: African Caribbean Attainment Project.

Alibhai-Brown, Y. (2001) *Mixed Feelings: The Complex Lives of Mixed-race Britain*, London: The Women's Press.

Arnot, M., McIntyre, D., Pedder, D. and Reay, D. (2004) *Consultation in the Classroom: Developing Dialogue About Teaching And Learning*, London: Pearson Publishing.

Audit Commission (2004) *The Journey To Race Equality: Delivering Improved Services to Local Communities*, London: Audit Commission.

BBC News.co.uk (2004) 'More Black teachers are needed', at http://news.bbc.co.uk/go/pr/fr/-/hi/england/london/3633026.stm, accessed on 7 September 2004.

BERA (British Educational Research Organisation) (2003) 'OECD review of educational research in England', *Research Intelligence* (82), pp. 25–26.

Ball, S. (1987) *The Micro-politics of the School: Towards a Theory of School Organisation*, London: Methuen and Co.

Ball, S. (1990) 'Educational markets, choice and social class: the market as a class strategy in the UK and the USA', *British Journal of Sociology of Education*, 14(1), pp. 3–19.

Banks, J. (1993) 'Education and cultural diversity in the United States' in A. Fyfe and P. Figueroa (eds), *Education for Cultural Diversity: The Challenge for A New Era*, London: Routledge.

Bastiani, J. (1991) Home School Contract of Partnership, Newsletter 3, Summer 1991, London: RSA.

Bastiani, J. (1997) *Home and School in Multicultural Settings*, London: David Fulton.

Bastiani, J. (2000) 'Supplementary schooling in the CfBT/Lambeth EducationAction Zone' in J. Hallgarten, *Parents Exist, OK!*, London: IPPR.

Benady, J. (2001) 'What Choice?', *Guardian Education*, 27 February.

Bernstein, B. (1996) *Pedagogy, Symbolic Control and Identity: Theory, Research, Critique*, London: Taylor and Francis.

Bhatti, G. (1999) *Asian Children at Home and at School: An Ethnographic Study*, London: Routledge.

Blair, M. (2001) 'The education of Black children: why do some schools do better than others?' in R. Majors (ed.), *Educating our Black children: New Directions and Radical Approaches*, London: Routledge.

Blair, M. and Bourne, J. (1998) *Making the Difference: Teaching and Learning Strategies in Successful Multi-ethnic Schools*, London: Department of Education and Employment/HMSO.

Bourdieu, P. (1986a) *The Field of Cultural Production*, Cambridge, UK: Polity Press.

Bourdieu, P. (1986b) 'The three forms of capital' in J. G. Richardson (ed.), *Handbook of Theory and Research for the Sociology of Education*, New York: Greenwood Press.

Bourdieu, P. and Passeron, J. C. (1977) *Reproduction in Education, Society and Culture*, London: Sage.

Bourne, J., Bridges, L. and Searle, C. (1994) *Outcast England – How Schools Exclude Black Children*, London: Institute of Race Relations.

Boushel, M. (1997) 'Vulnerable mixed race children: professional ideologies and parental realities', paper presented at the 'Rethinking Mixed Race' conference, National Institution for Social Work, London: December.

Brown, A. and Dowling, P. (1998) *Doing Research/Reading Research: A Mode of Interrogation for Education*, London: Falmer.

Bryan, B., Dadzie, S. and Scafe, S. (eds) (1985) *The Heart of the Race: Black Women's Lives in Britain*, London: Virago.

Bryman, A. (1988) *Quantity and Quality in Social Research*, London: Unwin Hyman.

Burgess, R. G. (ed.) (1985) *Issues in Educational Research: Qualitative Methods*, London: Falmer Press.

Callender, C. (1997) *Education for Empowerment: The Practice and Philosophies of Black Teachers*, Stoke-on-Trent: Trentham.

Centre for Contemporary Cultural Studies (1981) *Unpopular Education: Schooling and Social Democracy in England Since 1944*, Birmingham, UK: CCCS.

Centre for Public Policy Research (2000) 'Education Policy and Social Class', Kings College, London: July.

Chevannes, M. and Reeves, F. (1987) 'The Black voluntary school movement: definition, context and prospects' in B. Troyna (ed.), *Racial Inequality in Education*, London: Tavistock.

Clifford, J. (2000) 'Taking identity politics seriously: "The contradictory stony Ground ..."' in P. Gilroy, L. Grossberg and A. McRobbie (eds), *Without Guarantees: In Honour of Stuart Hall*, London: Verso.

Coard, B. (1971) *How the West Indian Child is Made Educationally Subnormal in the British School System*, London: New Beacon Books.

Coleman, J. S. (1990) *Foundations of Social Theory*, Cambridge, MA: Belknap.

Collins, P. H. (1996) *Black Feminist Thought*, London: Routledge.

Commission for Racial Equality (2003) *Toward Racial Equality: An Evaluation of the Public Duty to Promote Race Equality and Good Race Relations in England and Wales*, London: CRE.

Cork A. (2000) 'Racism: It's in the way', a poem in *Institutional Racism and the Police: Fact or Fiction*, London: Institute for the Study of Civil Society, pp. 17–18.

Cork, L. (2001a) 'Education and community action', *Education Action Research*, 9(3).

Cork L. (2001b) 'The class ceiling: Black families and their relationship with British schools', paper presented at AERA conference, Seattle, April.

Cork, L (2001c) Parent support organizations, African and Caribbean parents and home–school relations: Cultural-co-operation or cultural exclusion? University of Cambridge (unpublished doctoral thesis).

Crozier, G. (1996) 'Black parents and school relationships: A case study', *Educational Review*, 48(3), pp. 253–268.

Crozier, G. (1997) Review Symposium in *British Journal of Educational Studies*, 45 (4), pp. 416–419.

Crozier, G. (1998) 'Parents and schools: partnership or surveillance?', *Journal of Educational Policy*, 13(1), pp. 125–136.

Crozier, G. (1999a) 'Is it a case of "We know when we're not wanted"? The parents' perspective on parent–teacher roles and relationships', *Educational Researcher*, 41(3), pp. 315–328.

Crozier, G. (1999b) 'Parental involvement: Who wants it?', *International Studies in Sociology of Education*, 9(2), pp. 111–130.

Crozier, G. (2000) *Parents and Schools: Partners or Protagonists?*, Stoke-on-Trent: Trentham.

Cullingford, C. (1996) (ed.) *Parents, Education and the State*, Aldershot: Arena.

David, M. (1998) 'Home–school relations or families, parents and education', *British Journal of Sociology of Education*, 19(2), pp. 255–261.

David, M. (2000) 'Mothers' involvement in their children's schooling', paper presented at ESRC Seminar Series: 'Parents and Schools: Diversity, Participation and Democracy', Bath Spa University College: October.

Delpit, L. (1993) *Other People's Children: Cultural Conflict in the Classroom*, New York: The New Press.

DES (1991/1994) *The Parents' Charter*, London: HMSO.

Devine, F. (2004) *Class Practices: How Parents Help Their Children Get Good Jobs*, Cambridge: Cambridge University Press.

DfEE (1998a) *Teachers: Meeting the Challenge of Change*, London: HMSO.

DfEE (1998b) *Home School Agreements: What Every Parent Should Know*, London: HMSO.

DfEE (1999a) *Excellence in Schools*, London: HMSO.

DfEE (1999b) *Teachers Meet the Challenge: Education Action Zones*, London: HMSO.

DfES (2003) *Aiming High: Raising the Achievement of Minority Ethnic Pupils* (Ref: 0183/2003), Nottingham: DfES.

DfES/Desforges, C. with Abouchaar, A. (2003) *The Impact of Parental Involvement, Parental Support and Family Education On Pupil Achievement and Adjustment: A Literature Review* (RR433), Nottingham: DfES.

DfES (2004a) *Aiming High: Supporting Effective Use of EMAG* (Ref: DfES/0283/2004), London: DfES.

DfES (2004b) Minority Ethnic Exclusions and the Race Relations (Amendment) Act 2000, Research Report RR616.

Dillabough, J. (1997) Review Symposium in *British Journal of Educational Studies*, 45(4), pp. 409–415.

Drever, E. (1995) *Using Semi-structured Interviews in Small-scale Research: A Teacher's Guide*, Glasgow: The Scottish Council for Research Education.

Driver, G. (1982) 'Ethnicity and cultural competence, aspects of interaction in multiracial classrooms' in C. Bagley and G. K. Verma (eds), *Self Concept, Achievement and Multicultural Education*, London: Macmillan.

Edwards, A. (2002) 'Responsible research: ways of being a researcher', *British Educational Research Journal*, 28(2), pp. 157–69.

Ellis, B. (1995) *Schooling Black Children in Britain: A Practical Guide*, London: Ellis Publications.

Epstein, J. L. (1992) 'School and family partnerships', in M. C. Alkin (ed.), *Encyclopaedia of Educational Research* (6th edn 1139–1151), New York: MacMillan.

Epstein, J. and Sanders, M. (2000) 'Connecting home, school and community' in M. Hallinan (ed.), *Handbook of Sociology of Education*, pp. 285–306, New York: Klewer/Plenum.

Figueroa, P. (1993) 'Cultural diversity, social reality and education' in A. Fyfe and P. Figueroa (eds), *Education for Cultural Diversity: The Challenge for a New Era*, pp. 17–36, London: Routledge.

Foster, P., Gomm R. and Hammersley, M. (1996) *Constructing Educational Inequality: An Assessment of Research on School Processes*, London: The Falmer Press.

Foster, P., Gomm, R. and Hammersley, M. (1997) 'A response to the reviews', *British Journal of Educational Studies*, 45(4), pp. 406–408.

Fryer, P. (1984) *Staying Power: The History of Black People in Britain*, London: Pluto Press.

Garrison, L. (1993) 'A unique contribution: The Afro-Caribbean resource project' in A. Fyfe and P. Figueroa (eds), *Education for Cultural Diversity: The Challenge for a New Era*, pp. 267–274, London: Routledge.

Giddens, A. (1994) *Beyond Left and Right: The Future of Radical Politics*, Cambridge: Polity Press.

Gillborn, D. (1990) *Race, Ethnicity and Education*, London: Unwin and Hyman.

Gillborn, D. (1995) *Racism and Antiracism in Real Schools: Theory, Policy, Practice*, Buckingham/Milton Keynes: Open University Press.

Gillborn, D. (1996) *Exclusions From School*, Viewpoint series, no. 5, London: Institute of Education.

Gillborn, D. and Gipps, C. (1996) *Recent Research on the Achievements of Ethnic Minority Pupils*, London: HMSO.

Gillborn, D. and Mirza, H. (2000) *Educational Inequality: Mapping Race, Class and Gender: A Synthesis of Research Evidence*, London: HMSO/Ofsted.

Gilroy, P. (1987) *There Ain't No Black in the Union Jack*, London: Hutchinson.

Giroux, H. (1983) *Theory and Resistance in Education: A Pedagogy for the Opposition*, London: Heinemann Education.

Gramsci, A. (1971) *Selections from the Prison Notebooks*, London: Lawrence and Wishart.

Hall, S. (1986) 'Gramsci's relevance for the study of race and ethnicity', *Journal of Communication Inquiry*, 10(2), pp. 5–27.

Halpin, D. and Troyna, B. (1994) (eds) *Researching Educational Policy: Ethical and Methodological Issues*, London: Falmer Press.

Hammersley, M. (1995) *The Politics of Social Research*, London: Sage Publications.

Hammersley, M. (1997) 'Bias in social research', *Sociological Research*, 2(1), online at www.socresonline.org.uk.

Hart, S., Dixon, A., Drummond, M. J. and McIntyre, D. (2004) *Learning without Limits*, Berkshire: OUP/McGraw Hill Education.

Hayden, C. and Dunne, S. (2001) *Outside Looking In: Children's and Families' Experiences of Exclusion from School*, London: The Children's Society.

Hill Collins, P. (1990) *Black Feminist Thought: Knowledge, Consciousness and the Politics of Empowerment*, London: HarperCollins.

Home Office (2004) *ChangeUp: Capacity Building and Infrastructure Framework for the Voluntary and Community Sector*, London: Home Office.

hooks, b. (1989) *Talking Back: Thinking Feminist – Thinking Black*, Boston: Sheba.

Hughes, M., Wikely, F. and Nash, T. (1994) *Parents and Their Children's Schools*, Oxford: Blackwood.

Hulsebosch, P. (2000) 'Inviting families and community members to the table', paper presented at the AERA conference, New Orleans, April.

Hylton, C. (1999) *African Caribbean Community Organisation: The Search for Individual and Group Identity*, Staffordshire: Trentham Books.

John, G. (1999) 'The education of the Black child', paper presented at 'The Education of the Black Child' conference, London: February.

Johnson, D. and Ransome, E. (1980) 'Parents' perceptions of secondary schools' in M. Craft, J. Raynor and L. Cohen (eds), *Linking Home and Schools*, London: Harper and Row.

Jones, C., Maguire, M. and Watson, B. (1997) 'School experience of some ethnic minority students', *Journal of Education for Teaching*, 23(2), pp. 131–146.

Joseph Rowntree Foundation (2004) *Experiencing Ethnicity: Discrimination and Service Provision*, York, UK: Joseph Rowntree Foundation.

Lareau, A. (1989) *Home Advantage: Social Class and Parental Intervention in Elementary Education*, London: Falmer Press.

London Development Agency (LDA) (2004) *The Educational Experiences and Achievements of Black Boys in London*, London: LDA.

'London Schools and the Black Child' conference, London: March 2002, 2003; September 2004.

Mac an Ghaill (1988) *Young, Gifted and Black: Student–teacher relations in the Schooling of Black Youth*, Bucks: OUP.

Mac an Ghaill, M. (1991) 'Young, gifted and Black: methodological reflections of an action researcher', in G. Walford (ed.), *Doing Educational Research*, pp. 101–121, London: Routledge.

McCalla, D. (ed.) (2003a) *Black Success in the UK: Essays in Racial and Ethnic Studies*, London/Cambridge: Dmee/Cambridge University Press.

McCalla, D. (2003b) 'Syble's successful children', in D. McCalla (ed.), *Black Success in the UK: Essays in Racial and Ethnic Studies*, pp. 125–140, London/Cambridge: Dmee/Cambridge University Press.

McCarthy, C. (1998) *The Uses of Culture: Education and the Limits of Ethnic Affiliation*, New York/London: Routledge.

McGrath, A. and Woodhead, M. (eds) (1988) *Family, School and Society: A Reader*, London: Hodder & Stoughton/OUP.

McIntyre, D., Bhatti, G. and Fuller, M. (1993) *Educational Experiences of Ethnic Minority Students in the City of Oxford*, Oxford: Oxford University Department of Educational Studies.

Maclure, M. (1993) 'Arguing for your self: identity as an organizing principle in teachers' jobs and lives', *British Educational Research Journal*, 19(4), pp. 311–322.

McNamara, O., Hustler, D., Stronach, I. *et al.* (2000) Room to manoeuvre: mobilising the active partner in home–school relations', *British Educational Research Journal*, 26(4), pp. 473–490.

Macpherson, W. (1999) *The Stephen Lawrence Inquiry. Report of An Inquiry by Sir William McPherson of Cluny*, London: HMSO.

Majors, R. (ed.) (2001) *Educating our Black Children: New Directions and Radical Approaches*, London: Routledge.

Mercer, K. (2000) 'A sociology of diaspora' in *Without Guarantees: In Honour of Stuart Hall*, London and New York: Verso.

Mirza, H. (1997a) *Black British Feminism*, London and New York: Routledge.

Mirza, H. (1997b) 'Family matters in B. Cosin, and M. Hales, *Families, Education and Social Differences*, pp. 221–243, London: Routledge/OUP.

Mirza, H. (2000) 'Race, gender and IQ: the social consequences of a pseudo-scientific discourse' in K. Owusu (ed.), *Black British Culture and Society: A Text Reader*, London: Routledge.

Moore, D. (1999) paper of the same name presented at 'Educating the African Caribbean Child for Success: New Perspectives for the Year 2000' conference, Bedford: September.

Muir, H. (2004) 'No more lost boys', *The Guardian*, 7 September.

Munn, P. (ed.) (1993) *Parents and Schools: Customers, Managers or Partners*, London: Routledge.

Nehaul, K. (1996) *The Schooling of Children of Caribbean Heritage*, Stoke-on-Trent: Trentham.

NIACE (1997) *Learning to Live in a Multicultural Society: Home–School Liaison*, Leicester: NIACE.

Ofsted (1999) *Raising the Attainment of Minority Ethnic Pupils: School and LEA responses*, London: HMSO.

Ofsted (2002a) *Achievement of African Caribbean Pupils: Three Successful Primary Schools*, London: HMSO.

Ofsted (2002b) *Achievement of Black Caribbean Pupils: Good Practice in Secondary Schools*, London: HMSO.

Ofsted (2003) *Inspecting Schools: Framework for Inspecting Schools*, HMI 1523.

Ofsted (2004a) *Managing the Ethnic Minority Achievement Grant – Good practice in Primary Schools* (HMI 2072), London: HMSO.

Ofsted (2004b) *Managing the Ethnic Minority Achievement Grant – Good Practice in Secondary Schools* (HMI 2172), London: HMSO.

Osler, A. (1997) *Exclusion from School and Racial Equality*, London: Commission for Racial Equality.

Osler, A. (2000) (ed.) *Citizenship and Democracy in Schools: Diversity, Identity, Democracy*, Vol 1 and 2, Stoke-on-Trent: Trentham.

Osler, A. and Hill, J. (1999) 'Exclusions from school and racial equality: an examination of government proposals in the light of recent research evidence', *Cambridge Journal of Education*, 29(1), pp. 33–62.

Osula, B. (2004) *United We Stand, Divided We Fall – The ABCs of Success in Supplementary Education*, USA: Bramwell Osula.

Plowden Report (1967) *Children and Their Primary Schools*, Central Advisory Council for Education, London: HMSO.

Rampton, A. (1981) *West Indian Children in Our Schools*, Cmnd 8273, London: HMSO.

Reay, D. (1998) 'Engendering social reproduction: mothers in the educational market place, *British Journal of Sociology of Education*, 19(2), pp. 195–209.

Reay, D. (2001) 'Mothers' involvement in their childrens' schooling: social reproduction in action?', paper presented at ESRC Seminar Series: 'Parents and schools: diversity, participation and democracy', London: March.

Reay, D. and Mirza, H. S. (1997) 'Uncovering genealogies of the margins: Black supplementary schooling', *British Journal of Sociology of Education*, 18(4), pp. 476–500.

Richardson, R. and Wood, A. (1999) *Inclusive Schools, Inclusive Society*, Stoke-on-Trent: Trentham/Race on the Agenda/GLA.

Riley, K. (1994) *Quality and Equality: Promoting Equal Opportunities in School*, London: Falmer Press.

Rowntree Trust (1999) *Links Between School, Family and the Community: A Review of the Evidence*, Rowntree Trust: Findings Ref. N19.

Runnymede Trust, The (1998) *Improving Practice: A Whole School Approach to Raising the Achievement of African Caribbean Youth*, London/Nottingham: The Runnymede Trust/Nottingham Trent University.

Scarman, Lord (1981) *Report of an Inquiry into the Brixton Disorders*, pp. 10–12 London: HMSO.

Searle, C. (1996) 'OFSTEDed, Blunketted and permanently excluded: an experience of English education', *Race and Class*, 38, July–September, pp. 21–38.

Searle, C. (ed.) (1998) *Researching Society and Culture*, London: Sage.

Searle, C. (1999) *The Quality of Qualitative Research*, London: Sage.

Sewell, T. (1997) *Black Masculinities and Schooling: How Black Boys Survive Modern Schooling*, London: Trentham Books.

Sewell, T. and Majors R. (2001) 'Black boys and schooling: an intervention framework for understanding the dilemmas of masculinity, identity and underachievement' in R. Majors (ed.), *Educating our Black Children: New Directions and Radical Approaches*, London: Routledge.

Shaw, M. (2003a) 'Alarm at results of Black students', *TES*, March 7.

Shaw, M. (2003b) 'Everyone blames each other – and the rappers', *TES*, 7 March 7, p. 9.

Smith, D. J. (1997) *Racial Disadvantage in Britain*, Harmondsworth: Penguin.

Smith, R. (1998) *No Lessons Learnt: A Survey of School Exclusions*, London: The Children's Society.

Solomos, J. (1986) *Riots, Urban Protest and Social Policy: The Interplay of Reform and Social Control*, University of Warwick, Centre for Research in Ethnic Relations, Policy Papers in Ethnic Relations, No 7.

Spradley, J. P. (1979) *The Ethnographic Interview*, New York: Holt, Rinehart and Winston.

Stone, M. (1981) *The Education of the Black Child in Britain: The Myth of Multiracial Education*, Glasgow: Fontana.

Swann, Lord (1985) *Education for All: Final Report of the Committee of Inquiry into the Education of Children Ethnic Minority Groups*, Cmnd 9453, London: HMSO.

Tikly, L., Caballero, L., Haynes, J. and Hill J. (2004) *Understanding the Educational Needs of Mixed Heritage Pupils*, Bristol/Birmingham: University of Bristol/Birmingham Local Education Authority.

Tomlinson, S. (1985) 'The Black education movement' in M. Arnot (ed.), *Race and Gender: Equal Opportunities Policies in Education*, pp. 65–80, Oxford: Pergamon Press /OUP.

Tomlinson, S. (1997) 'The UK: An overview of the UK experience of home-school liaison', Summary of a presentation at Goldsmith's College, University of London, in *Learning to Live in a Multi-cultural Society: Home-School Liaison*, Leicester: NIACE, pp. 14–21.

Tomlinson, S. (2000) 'Ethnic minorities and education: New disadvantages', in C. Cox (ed.), *Combating Educational Disadvantage*, London: Falmer Press.

Vincent, C. (1996) *Parents and Teachers: Power and Participation*, London: The Falmer Press.

Vincent, C. (2000) *Including Parents?*, Milton Keynes: Open University Press.

Walker, B. M. and Maclure, M. (2001) *Home School Partnership in Practice*, ESRC Seminar Series, Parents and Schools: Diversity, Participation and Democracy, University of East Anglia, June.

West, A., Noden, P. and Edge, A. with David, M. (1998) 'Parental involvement in education in and out of school', *British Educational Research Journal*, 24(4), pp. 461–484.

Williams, C. (1995) 'How Black children might survive education' in M. Griffiths and B. Troyna, *Antiracism, Culture and Social Justice in Education*, London: Trentham.

Wright, C. (1987) 'Black students – white teachers' in B. Troyna (ed.) *Racial Inequality in Education*, London: Tavistock.

Wright, C., Weekes, D. and McLaughlin, A. (2000) *'Race', Class and Gender in Exclusion from School*, London: Falmer Press.

Young M. (1999) 'Multifocal educational policy research: Toward a method for enhancing traditional education policy studies' in *American Educational Research Journal*, 36(4), pp. 677–714.

Index

Abbott, D. 158
Abouchaar, 154, 160
academic ability 29–30
academic attainment 139
academic failure 148
academic progress 25, 51
academic records 19
academic support 72–3
ACER (African Caribbean Education
   Resource) centre 7
achievement 18, 24, 41–2, 59, 117,
   148
achievement session 27–8, 36, 44, 46,
   148
Actdale school 19–28
Actionaid 4–5, 47–60, 129, 131–2,
   134, 137–9, 143–4, 148, 154, 161;
   absence of teachers 55–6;
   chairperson 48–9; constitution 48;
   constraining factors 58; context and
   rationale of project 47; culturally
   specific support 52; education and
   school processes 50–1; environment
   55, 60; especially for Black parents
   49–50, 52; future of the
   organisation 58; how the
   organisation was established 48–9;
   implications for community-based
   organisations 59–60; implications
   for schools 58–9; key issues arising
   49–58; management committee
   48–9; minutes, agendas and reports
   58; need to know 49–53; parents'
   participation 57; resources 58;
   setting up the group 47–8; sharing
   perspective 54–5; teacher
   involvement 55–6; underlying
   matters 51

Actmount school 28–32, 147
advocacy 4, 82–109, 131; definition
   82; training in action 93–4; vs.
   mediation 83
Advocaid 4–5, 77, 82–109, 129–32,
   134–7, 141, 147, 150, 152, 155,
   161; case histories 83–92; gender
   issues 103–4; impact of support
   105–6; implications for schools
   107; implications for the
   organisation 109; key themes and
   issues 96–106; organisational
   culture 99–100; rationale 82; victim
   of own success 99; volunteers 99;
   workshops and conference
   presentations 94–6
African Caribbean Achievement Project
   (ACAP) 110–12, 116–17, 120–1,
   124, 126, 137, 156
agency/structure dilemmas 14
aggravation 140
aggression 34–5
*Aiming High: Raising the Achievement
   of Minority Ethnic Pupils* 12, 156
Althusser, L. 139
Arnot, M. 149
arrogance 101, 105
Asian children at home and at schools
   158
Asian parents 123
assertiveness 101
attendance pattern 22
attitude 29, 32–3, 41–2
Audit Commission 156

Bastiani, J. 12–13
behaviour 21–3, 26, 38, 42–3, 107,
   136, 150